HOW [illegible] LD NAPKINS

ANONYMOUS

ZINC READ

Published by
This edition copyright © 2024 by Zinc Read
Design and setting By Zinc Read
Email- zincread@gmail.com
ISBN-978-93-6768-369-9

CONTENTS

INTRODUCTION.

The folding of the serviette may often be made complimentary to the guest. Not only does "the Bridal" point out its special application; but "the Crown," "the Prince of Wales's Feather," and "the Mitre." "The Boat" is appropriate when a naval chief is the honored guest; "the Colonne de Triomphe," for the entertainment of a hero fresh from a new victory; "the Victoria Regia" for a distinguished botanist, and "the

Fan" for a reigning belle, so may "the Cocked Hat" be made available when a military hero is entertained, and "the Heraldic Rose" for a guest whose hobby is with things that appertain to the board.

In the days of our forefathers the quantity and quality of the viands were thought of more consideration than the appointments of the table.

Provided the hospitable board groaned beneath the combined weight of

substantial food and a silver service, the banquet was pronounced

magnificent. Now we have changed all that. The contents of the dishes have become secondary in importance to the decorations. The eye must be feasted as well as the palate. Heavy silver ornaments have given place, or at least are associated with, vases of crystal and abundance of flowers, with scent fountains and the choice fruit selected for dessert. The folding of the serviette, or table napkin, was always a matter of attention; at the present moment it is doubly so, when the luxury of table decorations are carried to such an extent that ingenuity is constantly on the strain, not only to produce every

possible variety of *cartes de menu*, but even fanciful stands to hold them or the guests' name-cards in a prominent position. The parlor maid or the waiter, or the dainty mistress of the house herself, must look to their laurels in the matter of folding serviettes, or the other showy trifles placed on the board will cast the attractions of the table napkin completely into the shade. To fold them well in the more elaborate styles, it is necessary that they should be made of very fine, but rather stout damask, starched more or less, quite fresh and nearly new. Old damask, that is soft, will not take the more elaborate forms. Each serviette, previous to folding it, should be laid on the ironing-board damped with (raw) starch, smoothed with a hot iron, and immediately folded whilst crisp and steaming. It not only folds better, but preserves the form longer by such means; and unless this is attended to designs like "the Fan," "the

Victoria Regia," "the Bridal," and "the Colonne de Triomphe," could not effectually be made.

"The Boat" and "the Basket" also require very stiff serviettes. The serviettes must be exactly square, and pains taken to make the sides perfectly even and true.

FOLDING SERVIETTES.

THE ESCUTCHEON.

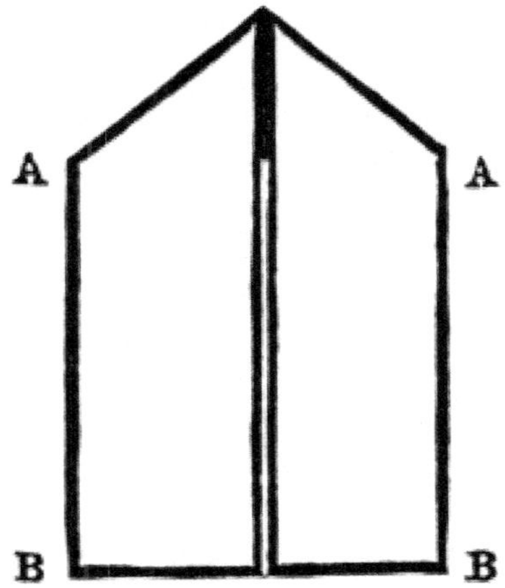

Fig. 1.

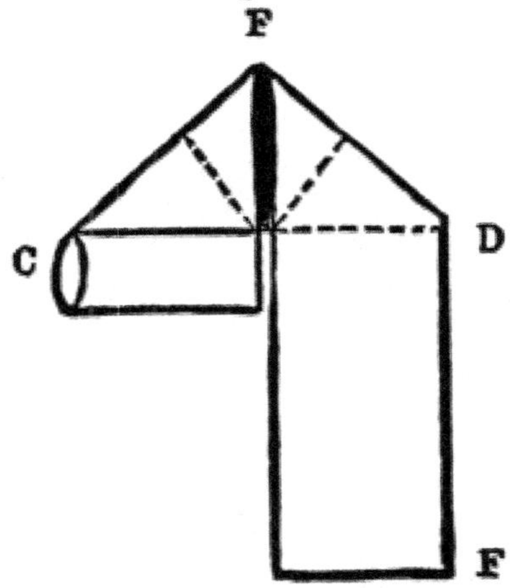

Fig. 2.

This is one of the easiest methods possible of ornamentally folding a serviette, and we recommend a novice to commence with it. Indeed, we have arranged the folding as progressively as possible. Although it will sit more crisp and fresh in appearance if made with a fine new well starched material, the Escutcheon can be made very well with old or even crumpled damask, though, of course, serviettes should always be scrupulously clean and smooth. First, fold the serviette in half lengthwise; and then fold it in half again lengthwise, keeping the edges to the lower end, which comes where in the diagram A A and B B are marked (see fig. 1). It is necessary to be always very precise in making the folds, bringing the edges and corners exactly to meet, a rule which applies to all the designs; but without strict attention to which, the more elaborate patterns cannot be represented.

Now turn over each end of the serviette (which you have already folded in four), in the manner shown in fig. 1, creasing it quite flat. Then take one of the ends and roll it up in the manner shown in fig. 2, from C to D. Take the other end, E, and roll it in the same way. It is to be observed that these rolls are brought exactly to meet (not to overlap) the triangle formed at the top. It is, however, necessary to remark that the napkin is to be rolled in the reverse way from that apparent in the illustration; that is, to be rolled *under* and not *over*, a difference which must not be neglected. Keep the rolls one in each hand, and with a twist of the wrist bring over the roll C, to the point F (causing the fold marked by the dotted line), and with a twist of the other wrist bring the roll up to the same point to match it. Then lay it flat on the table, the rolls underneath (see fig. 3), and keeping them down with the hand, raise the other part and shape it as shown in fig. 4, and slip the dinner roll in the hollow at the back.

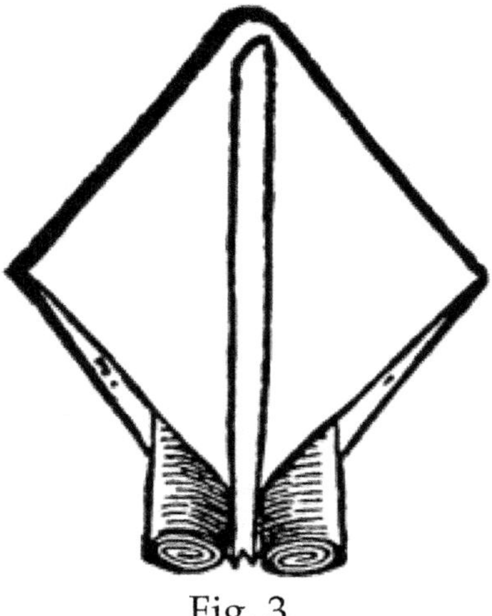

Fig. 3.

Fig. 4.

THE CHESTNUT POCKET.

Fig. 1.

Fig. 2.

Fold the serviette in half both ways, and open it again. Bring all the corners to the centre. Turn it over and again bring all the corners to the centre. Turn it back again and slip the chestnuts in the four pockets to be observed in fig. 1.

Fig. 2, the Pocket Serviette, is made in the same way; but the corners are brought three times, instead of twice, to the centre, turning it each time (see fig. 2).

THE SHIELD.

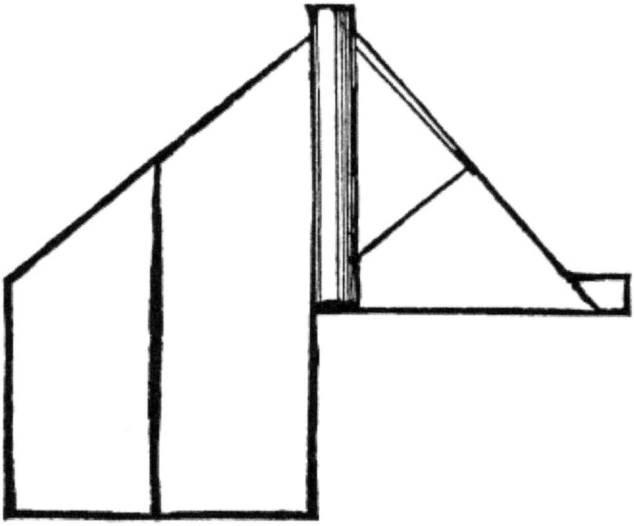

Fig. 1.

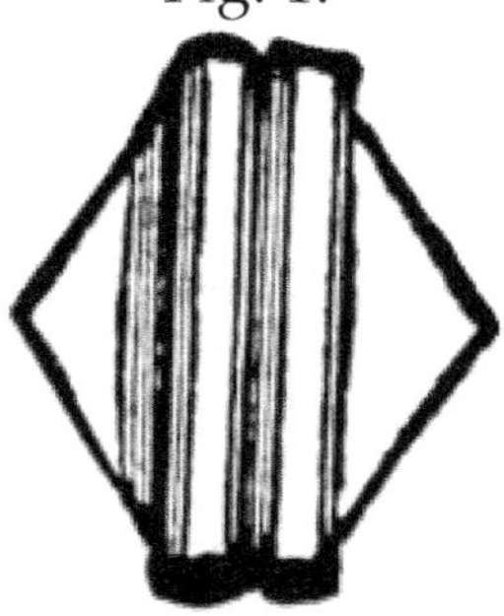

Fig. 2.

The Shield is almost identical with the Escutcheon; there is, however, a slight difference, which forms a little variety and practice in the art of napkin-folding.

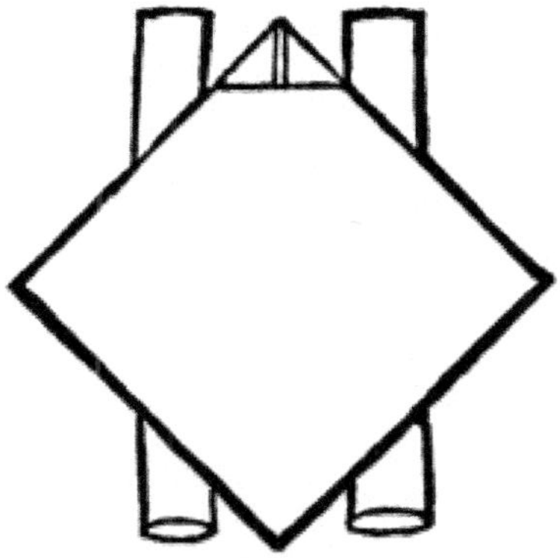

Fig. 3.

Fig. 4.

First form fig. 1, as for the Escutcheon. Next roll up the two ends in the manner shown in fig. 2; that is, make the rolls outwardly, not under as in the previous direction. The serviette will now resemble fig. 3. Then set it into form, and place the bread inside. The face of it will stand perfectly upright and resemble figure 4.

THE MITRE.

The Mitre is a well-known device, and one which always looks effective. It is not unlike the Crown. Fold the damask in half, and turn down the two corners to meet at both ends, in the manner shown in fig. 1, taking care to let them meet very exactly and not overlap. Fold it in half at the line A to B, fig. 1, to ascertain the centre. Open this last fold again and bring the two points to the centre like fig. 2. Fold these together at the dotted line with the points *outside*, let down one of these corners again, and turn in the two points A and B also, to make a triangle uniform with the others: it will now resemble fig. 3. Turn the serviette over; let down the point on that side: it will then resemble fig. 4. Turn in the corners A and B, by the line marked. Turn up the point D to its former position: it will now resemble fig. 5. Slip the hand inside the hollow to be found at the broad end, and shape it like a cap, and the Mitre is complete.

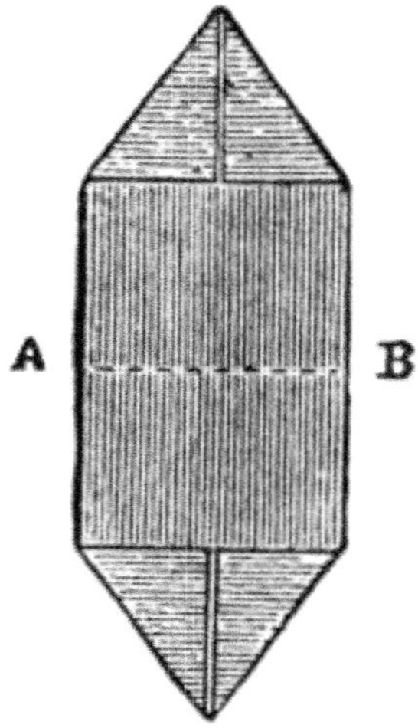

Fig. 1.

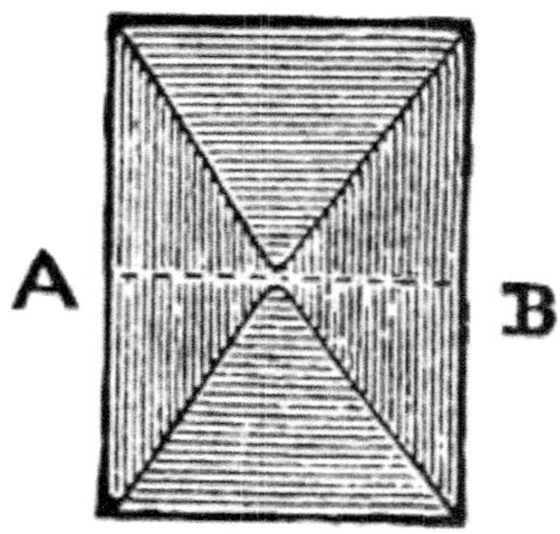

Fig. 2.

Fig. 3.

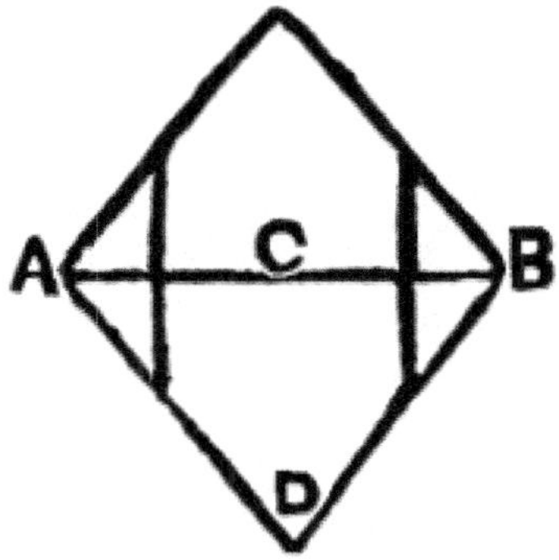

Fig. 4.

Fig. 5.

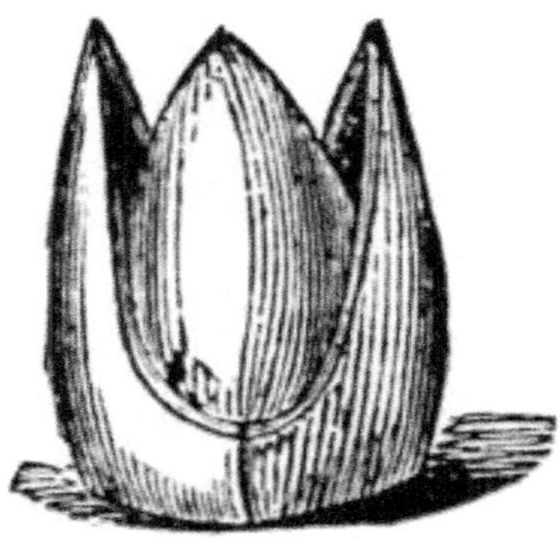

Fig. 6.

THE CORNUCOPIA.

Cornucopias are easily folded, and very effective down a long dinner table, with a single scarlet geranium flower at the apex of each. Halve the serviette lengthways; turn down the corners at the two ends to meet in the centre and form a triangle, like fig. 4, in the Crown. Take the corners at the base and bring them to the apex, like fig. 1. Then double it together with folds inside: it will now appear like fig. 2. At the side marked A, there are three folds. Set it upright over the dinner roll, with two of these folds one side and one on the other. Shape it nicely, keeping the space from B to C close.

Fig. 1.

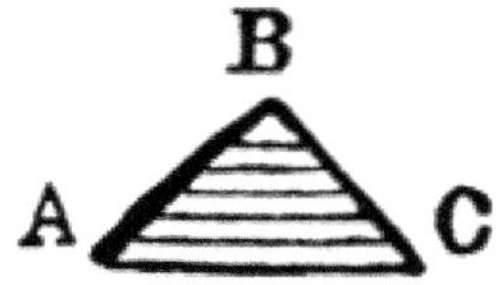

Fig. 2.

Fig. 3.

THE CROWN.

This is a handsome design, and is one which requires very well starched damask. The bread is placed inside, underneath the crown. Now that flowers are so much used, nothing could have a more charming effect than a slight wreath of flowers round the base of it, at the part marked A to B, in fig. 1. Fig. 2 represents the serviette laid on the table. Fold it exactly in half from A to B, open and fold the reverse way, from C to D. Open it again. These creases are merely made to ascertain the true centre. At it lies, turn all the points to the centre, and crease down in the manner observed in fig. 3, which forms a diamond. Take the four corners of the diamond and fold them to the centre again. The serviette will still preserve the shape shown in diagram fig. 3, but be smaller in size. Bring the top, A, to the right hand, B, and the left hand, B, to the other, A; it will now resemble Fig. 4. Fold down the corners, E F and G H, parallel to the line I J; it will now resemble fig. 5. Put the hand inside it at the broad end, and shape it like a cap, over the hand, folding one end into the other as shown at C, in fig. 5, The stiffness of the damask should be sufficient to keep these last folds in place; the corner fold should just be turned one corner within the other as an envelope, and pinched, to secure its remaining firm.

Fig. 1.

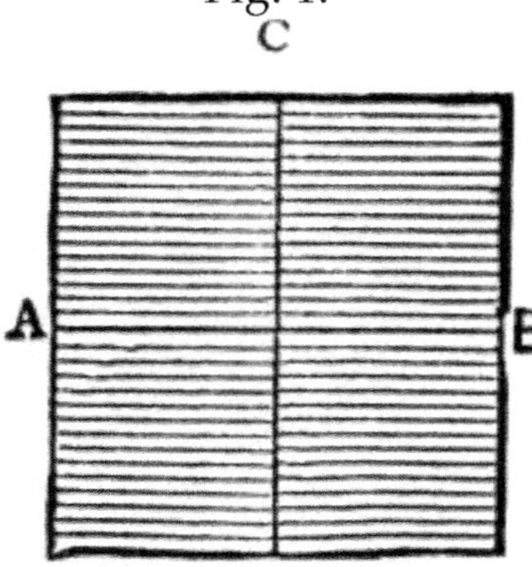

Fig. 2.

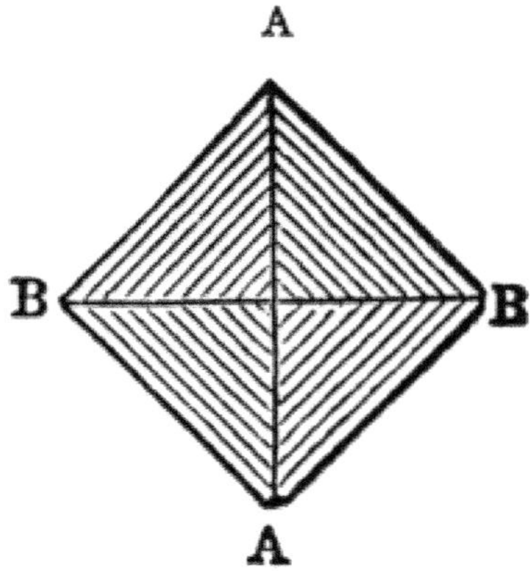

Fig. 3.

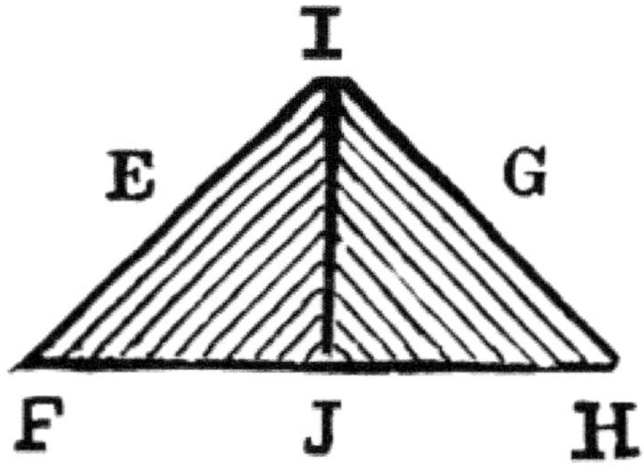

Fig. 4.

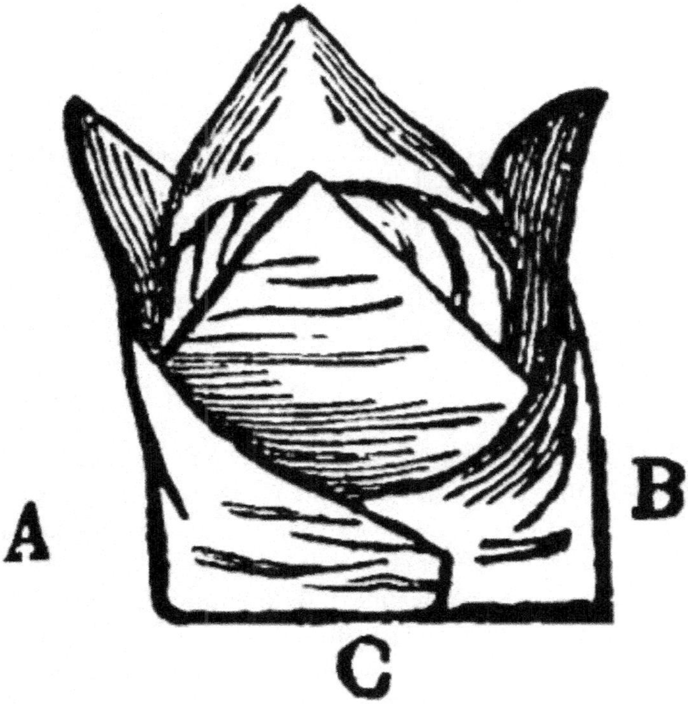

Fig. 5.

THE SCROLL.

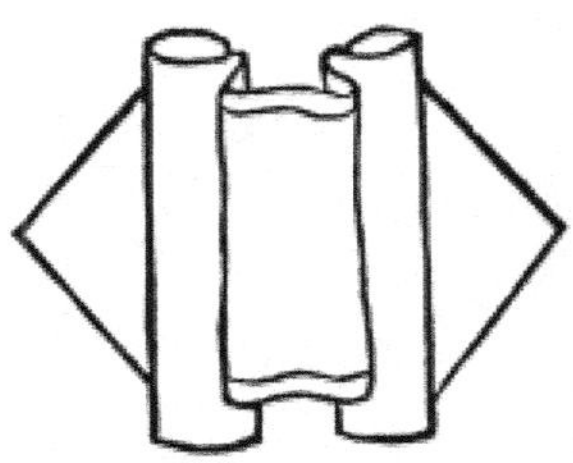

Fig. 1.

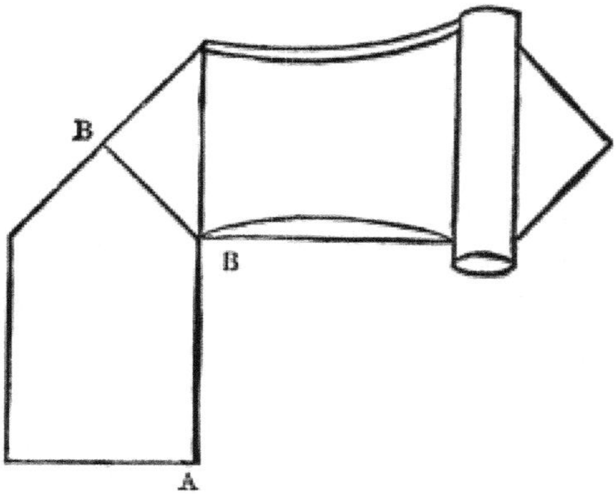

Fig. 2.

The Scroll is simple to fold. It is represented complete (fig. 3). The bread is under the centre, on which the name card may be laid. It does not require to be stiff. First fold the serviette four times lengthways. Fold down one end in the manner shown at A, in fig. 2. Then fold the end A completely across, forming the line, B B. Roll up the end A, and produce the fig. 3. Treat the other side in the same way. Fig. 3 illustrates the process. The space in the middle, A, fig. 1, is closed over the bread.

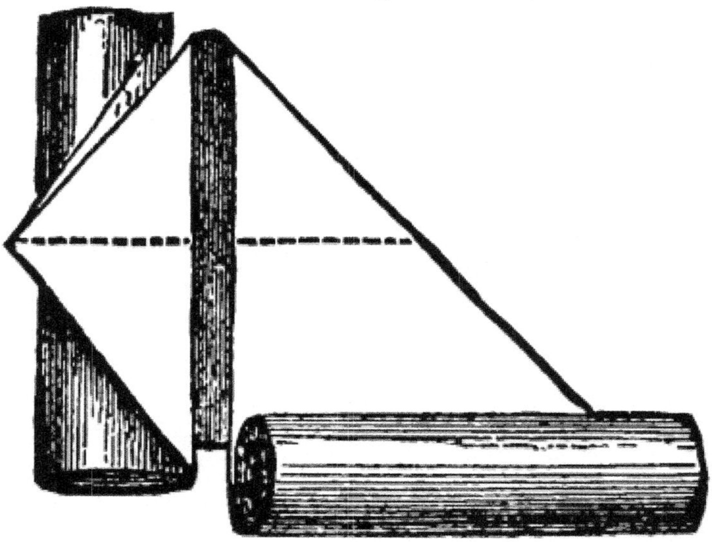

Fig. 3.

THE SLIPPERS.

Fig. 1.

Fig. 2.

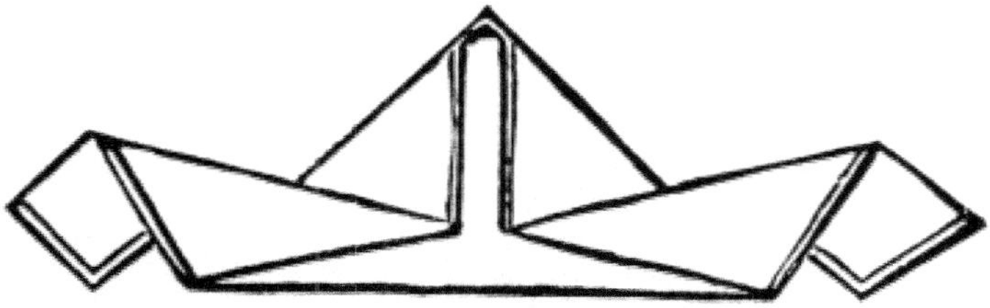

Fig. 3.

The Slippers are very easy to make. Double the serviette four times lengthways. Then fold like fig. 1. The ends are simply rolled, taking the corners in the method shown in fig. 2; bringing them over as shown in fig. 3, and with another turn forming the Slippers (fig. 4). Secure the point at A, with the left hand, whilst rolling up the other side; and then hold both points together with the left hand and place the right in the top of the Slippers, setting them over the dinner roll, which should be placed underneath at B, fig. 4; and the Slippers pinched close together at the top over it. A few flowers in the hollows of the folds is a pretty addition.

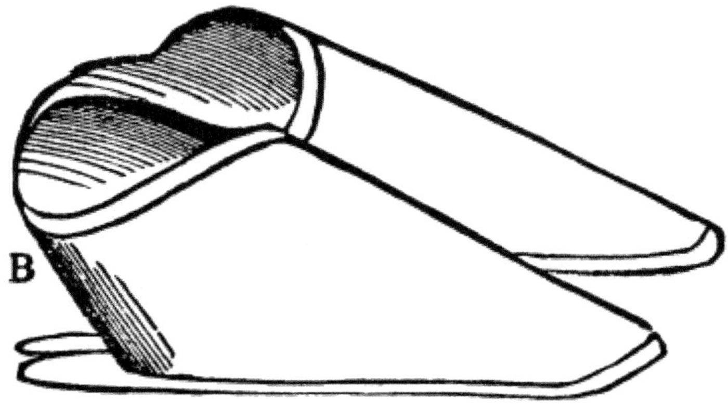

Fig. 4.

THE COCKED HAT, OR BOAT.

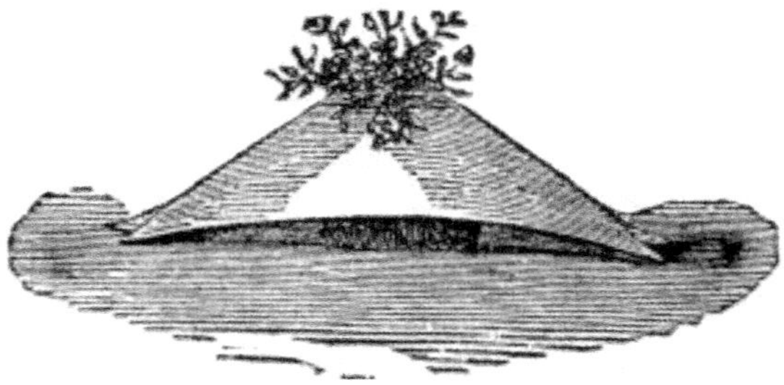

Fig. 6.

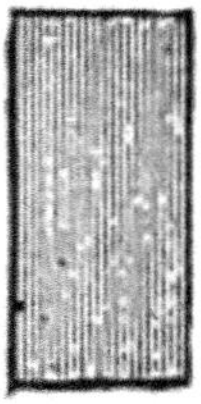

Fig. 1.

Fig. 2.

Fold a serviette in half lengthways (see fig. 1), then in half again (fig. 2). Fold it lengthways again, with the edges-inside, in the way shown in fig. 3. Fold it in half lengthways at the dotted line with the edges outside.

Turn down the corners in the manner explained by fig. 4, both sides alike; it now resembles fig. 5. Turn in the superfluous end C, shown in fig. 4, inside the hat: this makes it resemble fig. 6. Shape it with the hand and slip it over the dinner bread. If the edges are left outside in folding (fig. 3), when finished, a space will be offered at the top wherein a few flowers may be placed. A Boat may also be folded by this diagram by reversing its position on the plate. A still better way to make the Boat is to double a serviette in half lengthways, and again the reverse way. Fold the two edges to the centre: this makes an oblong. Turn it over on the other side. Turn two of the corners to meet in the centre; must not be opposite corners, but both at the right end. Turn the two left end corners half to the middle. Iron down. Then fold the whole in half lengthways, having the corners inside. This completes the Boat. Put the bread underneath.

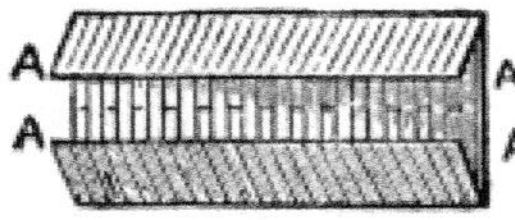

Fig. 3.

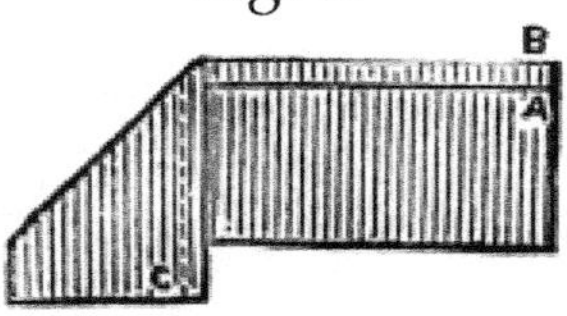

Fig. 4.

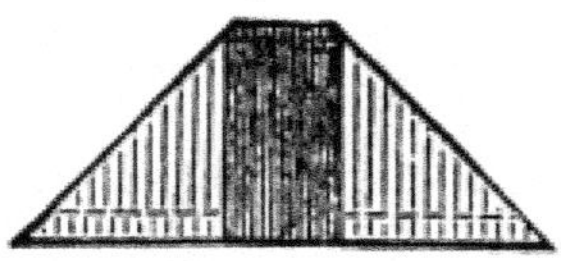
Fig. 5.

ANOTHER BOAT.

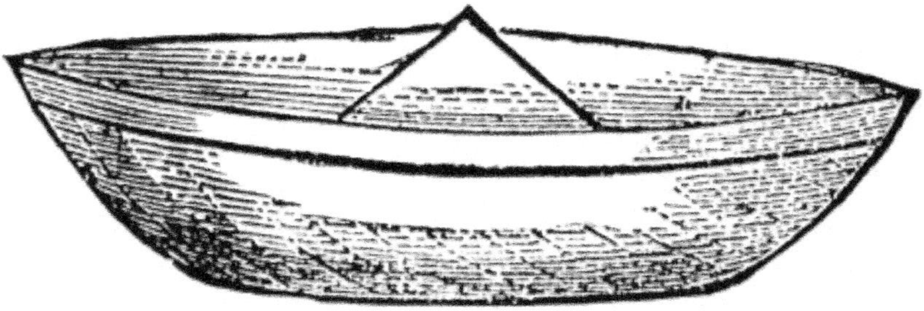

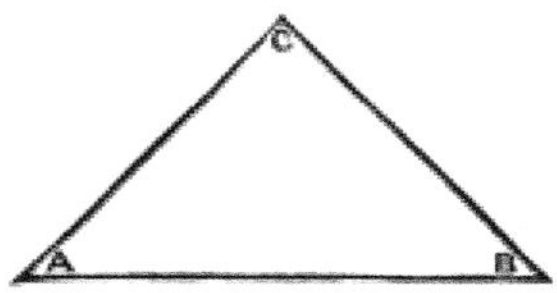

Fig. 1.

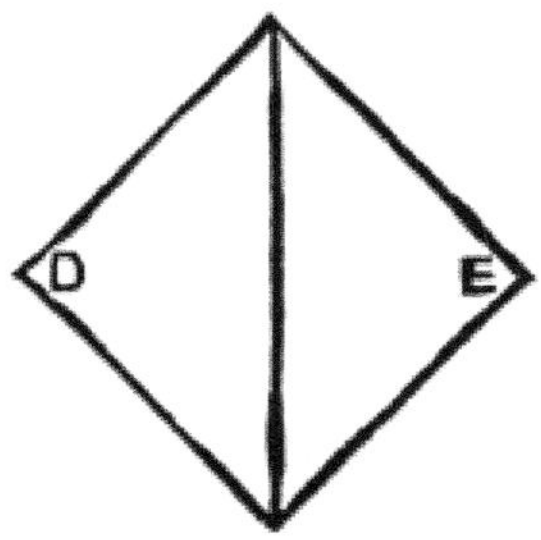

Fig. 2.

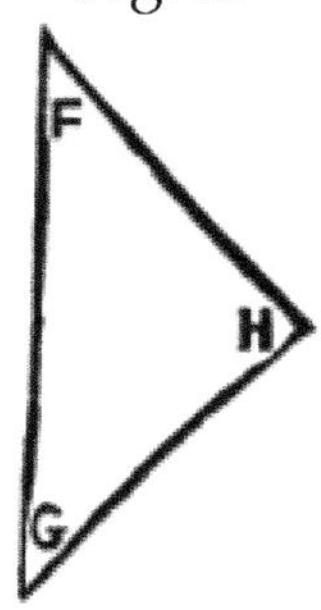

Fig. 3.

The Boat is exceedingly pretty, especially if freighted with a few flowers. The serviette should be well starched to sit firm and sharp, and must be an exact square. First fold it in half like a shawl. Next take the corner A (fig. 1), and bring it to C. Turn over the serviette on the other side. Take the corner B, and bring it to C in the same way, but on the other side: this forms fig. 2. Fold fig. 2 in half by the line in the centre, bringing D to E, and forming fig. 3. Fold the point F to H. Turn over the serviette and fold G to H, on the other side; this produces fig. 4. Fold the half of the end J to K, producing fig. 5. Fold L to K, on the other side. These folds must be so made as to leave the upper part of the serviette, which will now again open and look like fig. 3, from F to G. Slip the hand inside here, round it open a little, and so bring F to meet G, making it flat the reverse way: this is represented by fig. 6. Turn down the whole point M to N, on the thinnest side, like fig. 7. Slip in the thumbs at the opening at O in fig. 7, and holding the last fold firmly down; dexterously turning the Boat inside out: the inside fold resembles a capital A. Pinch the sides of the A the other way, making it an A again; and drawing out the Boat lengthways. Shape it a little with the hand. The bread may be slipped under the centre, A, or cabin of the Boat, provided it is not too large. A pretty addition to this would be to attach the *carte de menu*, by the means of a Chinese ribbon, to a chip, spill, or blender stick, and fix it in the Boat as a sail. The name card may also be attached to resemble an additional sail.

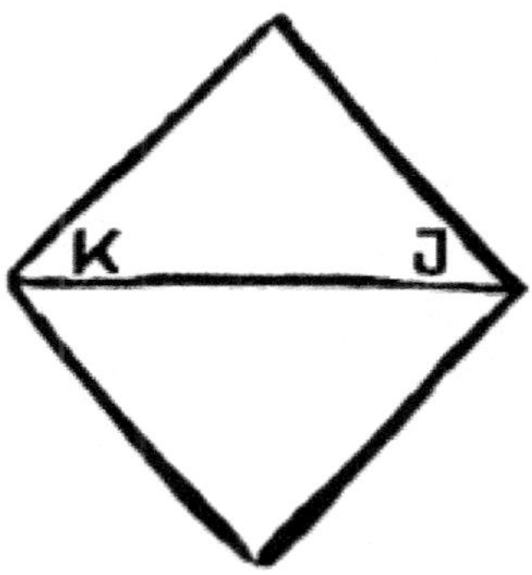

Fig. 4.

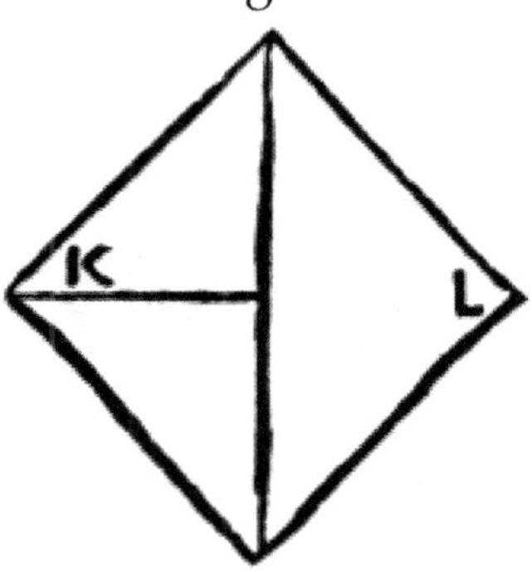

Fig. 5.

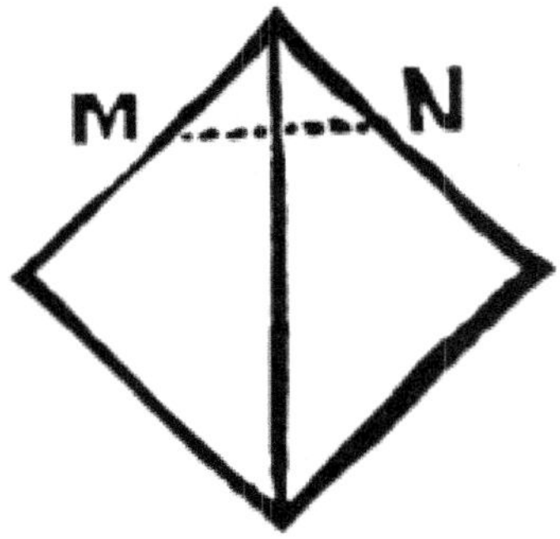

Fig. 6.

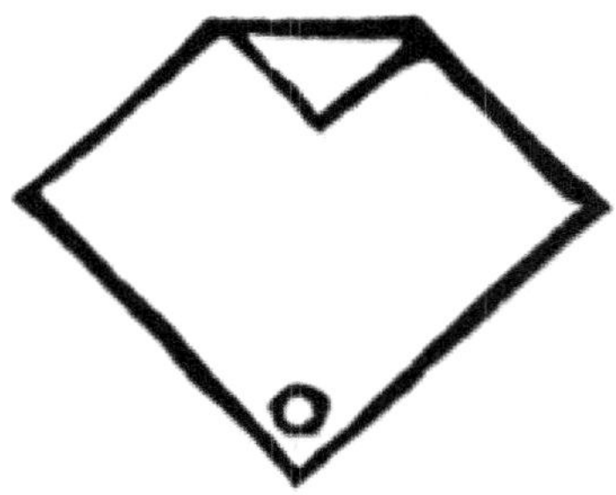

Fig. 7.

THE HAMBURG DRUM.

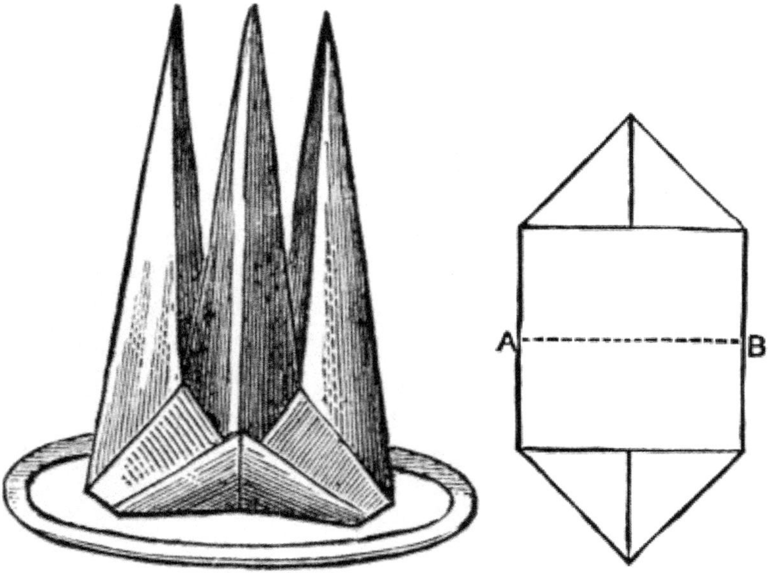

Fig. 1.

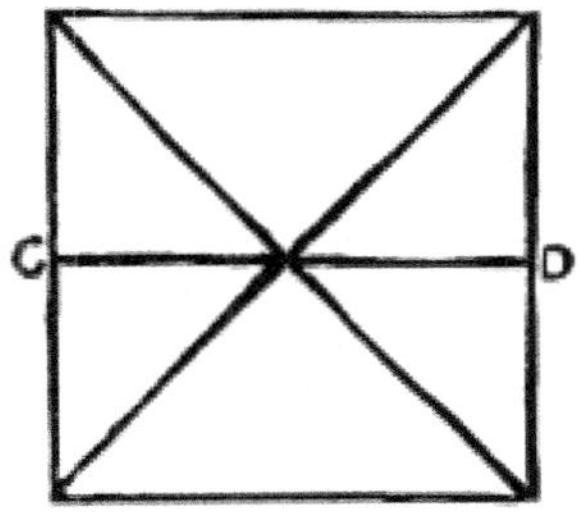

Fig. 2.

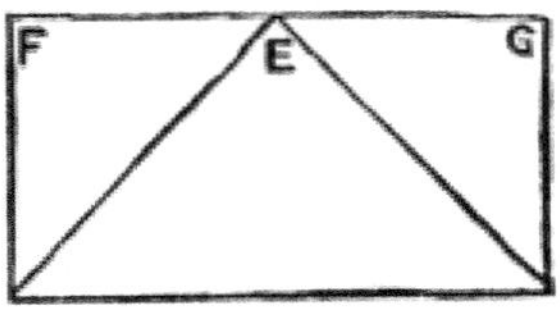

Fig. 3.

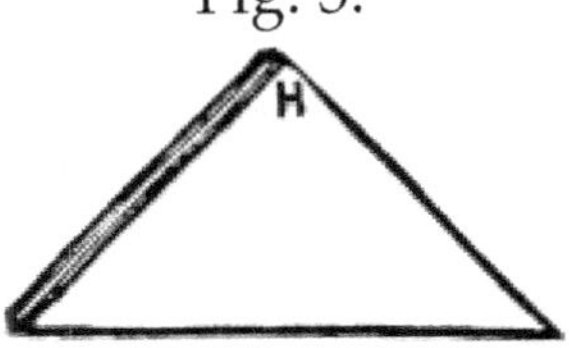

Fig. 4.

The first three folds are made like those of the Mitre; namely, fold the serviette in half lengthways. Turn down the corners like fig. 1, fold it in half across the centre, inwards, from A to B, keeping the corners inside. It will now resemble fig. 2. Fold it again from C to D, into the shape of fig. 3. Let down the point E; turn down the corners F and G, to make a triangle uniform with the others: thus you have fig. 4. Let down the corner H, as shown in fig. 5: this corner must be the one that has the selvage on the lower corner. Make the fold by the dotted line in fig. 5: this produces fig. 6. Take the upper fold at A and B in the same diagram, open it back and crease it down to resemble fig. 7; turn the napkin over. You now have fig. 8. Fold over the edges C and D to E, to match the folds on the other side. Turn up the napkin again; turn up the point C, and bring the corners, E and F, together likewise. Slip the hand into the hollow at the base, as you did for the Mitre; and place over the bread.

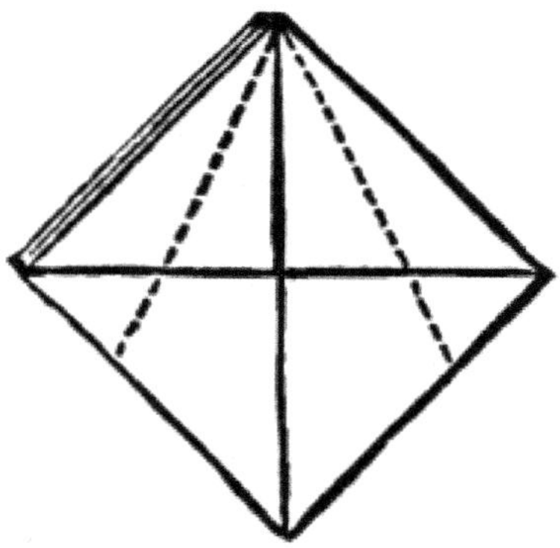

Fig. 5.

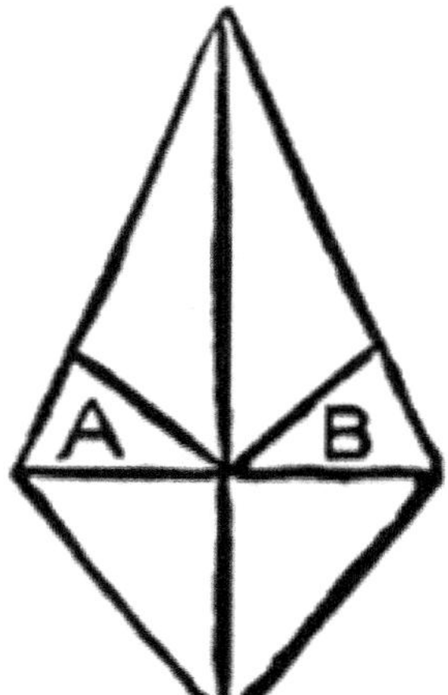

Fig. 6.

Fig. 7.

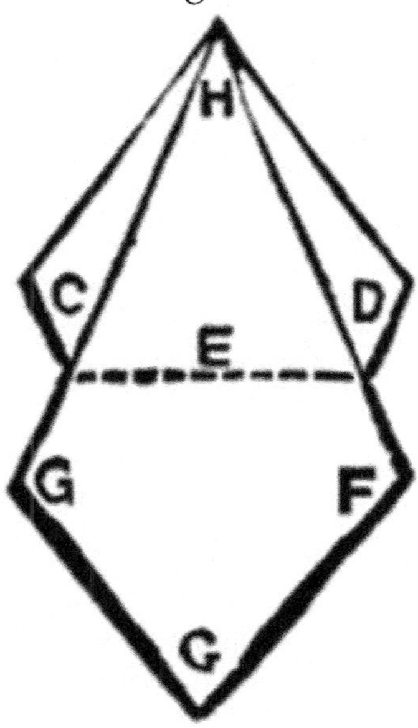

Fig. 8.

THE HERALDIC ROSE AND STAR.

Fig. 1.

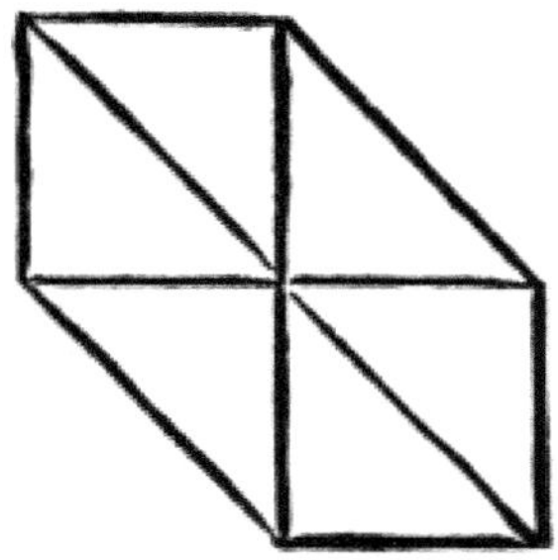

Fig. 2.

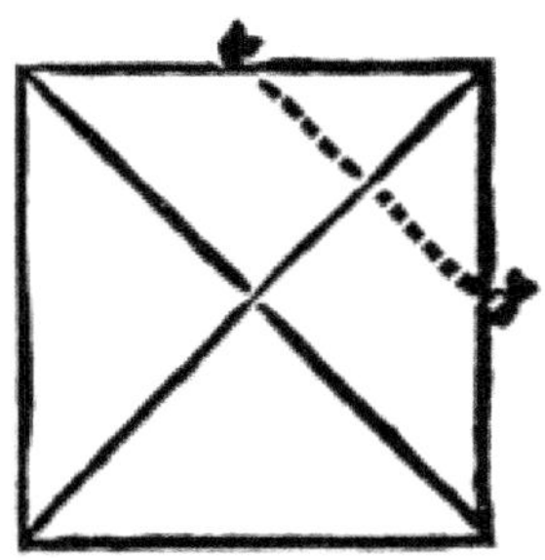

Fig. 3.

Spread a serviette, full size, flat on the table. It must be a perfect square, exact at the corners. Bring the four corners exactly to the centre, in the way described in fig. 1. Take the corners A and B, and without turning the serviette, again bring them to the centre, as shown in fig. 2. Bring C and D likewise to the centre: this forms fig. 3. Take one corner and turn it *under* (not over as before) by the dotted line *e* to *f*; turn under the other three the same way. Then again bring all the four corners to the centre, on the upper side, as in fig. 2.

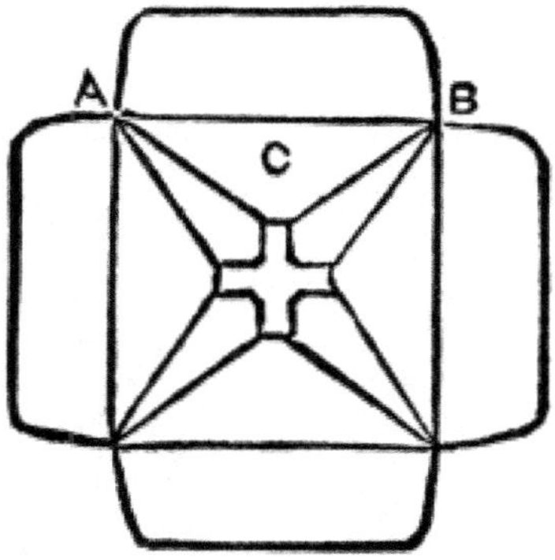

Fig. 4.

Fig. 5.

Afterwards repeat turning all the corners under, as in fig. 3. Then once more repeat fig. 2, and bring the remaining corners to the centre, uppermost. Press the folds firmly down. Then, one at a time, turn the corners half back, shaping them like little pockets, by slipping the fingers in at C (A to B, fig. 4), and forming the corners out square. This makes the Rose. Or by turning it down in the same way, without squaring out the corners, the Star, fig. 5, is made. Open up the eight petals, to be found in the centre, and fit in the dinner roll.

THE MINARETTES.

The Minarettes is a design expressly originated for the present work. It requires to be well stiffened. Fold the napkin in half. Turn down the corners as in fig. 1 of the Mitre. Fold in half and turn in the corners till you have an exact triangle as in the Mitre (see fig. 1). Then let down the outer side of the triangle. Fold the corners at both sides by the dotted lines, A and B (fig. 1). Take the outer pieces, C and D, and fold back so as to have two points alike. Fold the lower end to match; halve it, and you will now have fig. 2. Fold up at the dotted line. Pass the fold inside like fig. 3. Bend over the corners like fig. 4, and place the Minarettes over the roll.

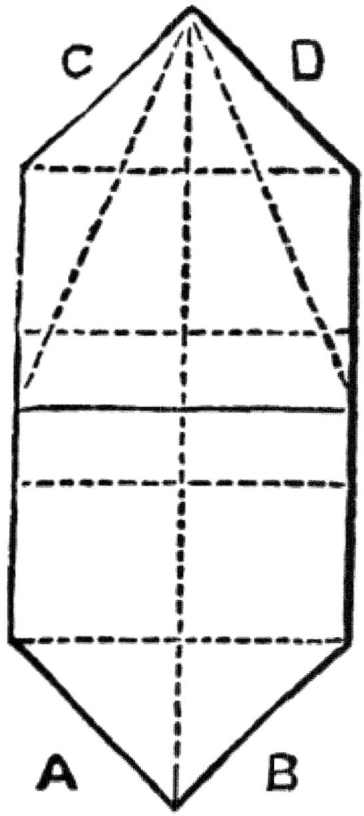

Fig. 1.

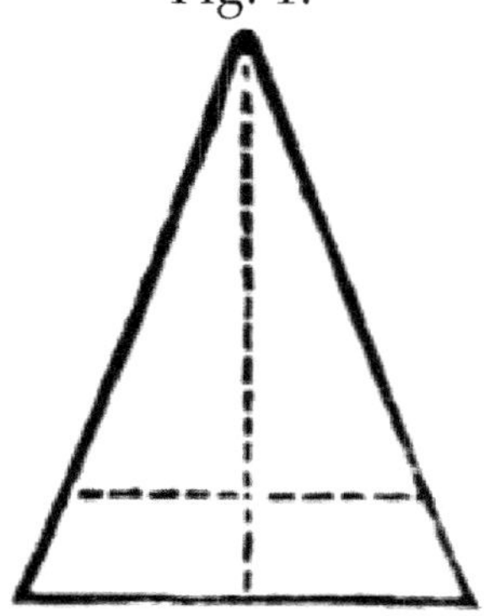

Fig. 2.

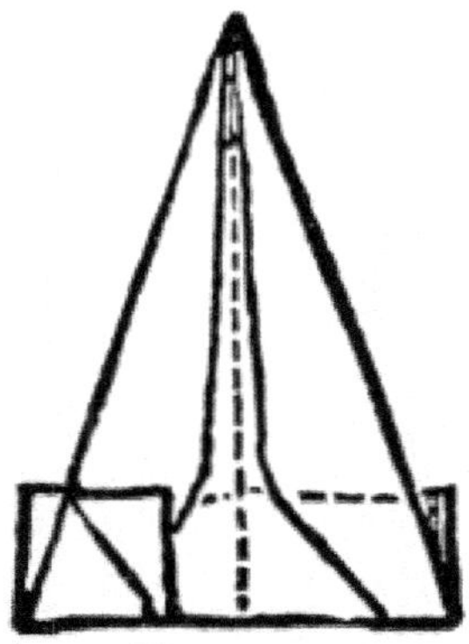

Fig. 3.

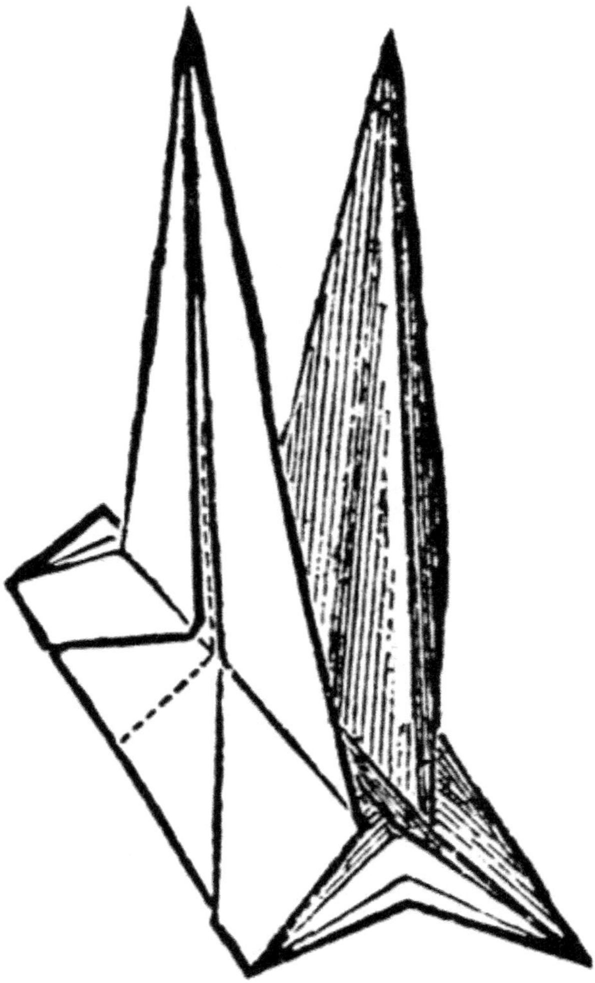

Fig. 4.

THE SHELL.

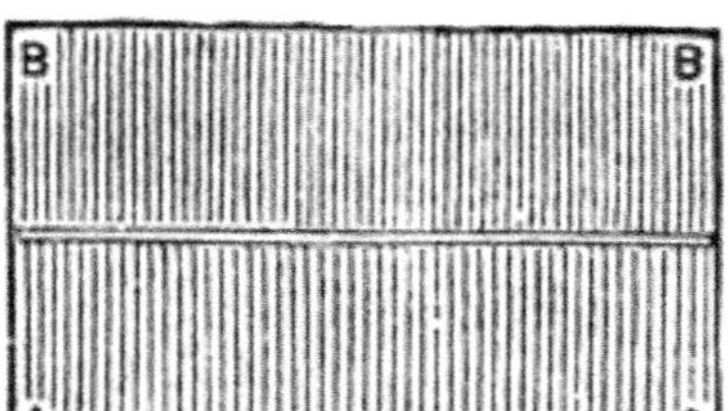

Fig. 1.

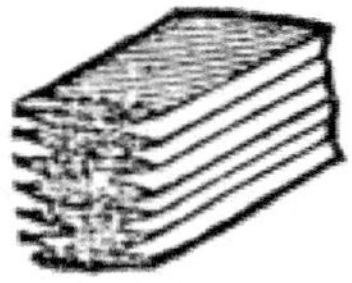

Fig. 2.

Fig. 3.

The Shell requires a very stiff serviette. Fold the two edges together in the centre, lengthways, as shown in fig. 1. Fold in half down the centre, also lengthways, leaving the edges outside. Then crimp evenly in the manner shown in fig. 2. Open up the top end, and turn down the edges each way, as they appear in fig. 3. Keep the lower ends together like a fan. If well done, it can be balanced on the plate by the ends, in the manner illustrated by fig. 4.

Fig. 4.

THE FAN.

Fig. 5.

The fan is made precisely like the Shell, only the edges are not turned down; but in folding, at first, are kept inside. The fan is placed in a glass, in the way shown in fig. 5.

It is, also, sometimes folded again before crimping three parts up. This forms a double Fan, and the lower one should be pulled out a little by the fingers.

THE ROSETTE FAN.

The Rosette Fan is very handsome and uncommon, but difficult to make, requiring very nice manipulation. First fold the serviette in half, lengthways, the edges downward. As it lays on the table, make it into three equal folds, lengthways. Then take the upper fold between the finger and thumb, lengthways, and the lower fold between the second and third fingers of each hand. Bring the lower fold up to within an inch and a half of the fold left, and the one between the finger and thumb to within an inch and a half of that. The hemmed edges ought to be an inch and a half below the last of the three plaits you have now formed. Press them well down. Crimp as for the Rosette. Hold what would be the handle of the Fan well in the left hand, and keep it all close together. Insert right through the upper fold or plait the handle of a silver fork, the flat way, and when right through, turn it, rounding out the plait like a bullionne on a lady's dress. Treat the other two plaits in the same way. Then put the handle end firmly in a glass and let the top spread out. The effect is excellent.

THE VICTORIA REGIA.

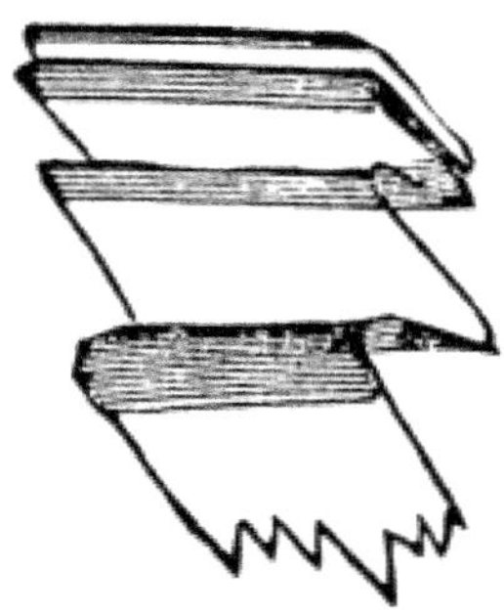

Fig. 1.

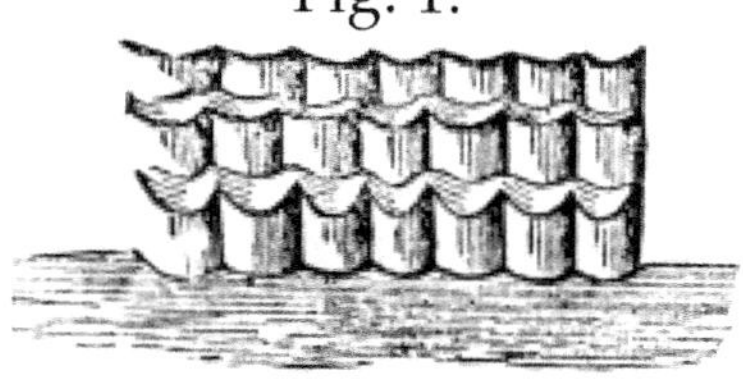

Fig. 2.

Fig. 3.

This spirited design is difficult to accomplish, and requires to be very stiff indeed. Fold the serviette in half twice, lengthways, keeping the hems to the edge. Then plait it as the Shell was plaited, in the way shown in fig. 1. The number of petals will depend on the number of folds, which should be twice as many as were made for the Shell, the width being only half as much. Keep the folds as close together as possible, and begin forming the petals by drawing back the first hem, as the edge of the Shell was done. Proceed to turn down the next fold and make another round of petals to meet the first ones, and finish by making the last hem fold in the same way (fig. 2). Set it round by bringing the two edges of the serviette together. It is not at all easy to set the petals well. The bread is not to be placed in or under it; but a single flower, such as a rose, may very properly be slipped into the heart. Fig. 3 represents the Victoria Regia, which should be placed in the centre of the plate.

THE SWAN.

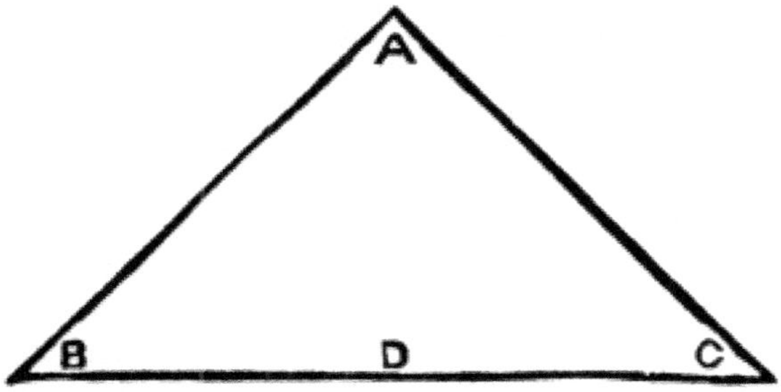

Fig. 1.

The Swan is a very simple fold, yet one requiring some knack to produce. The serviette should be very stiff. Form a triangle by folding it in half. Hold the point, A, between the teeth; take C and B in each hand. Hold it tight across the chest, so that from A to D it is strained tight against you. Roll up the ends B and C very tight, one in each hand, in the manner shown in fig. 2. The reason it is held tight across the chest is to keep it plain at E; otherwise it would curl up to the top. Now bring the points B and C together (fig. 2). Bend over the point A and shape the twisted pieces so as to give the appearance of a Swan. Our illustration gives but a rough notion of it, as it is not easy to delineate well on paper, and at the same time show the way of bending it. With a little manipulation, a very good imitation of a Swan may be produced. The centre piece is the head and neck; the twisted portions represent the outline of the breast, body and the legs.

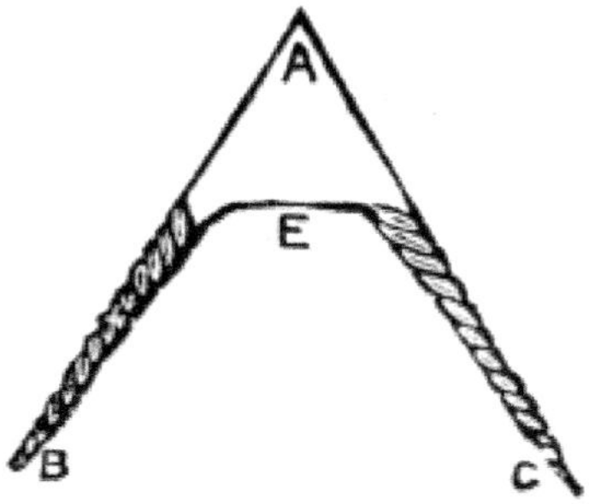

Fig. 2.

Fig. 3.

LORGNETTES.

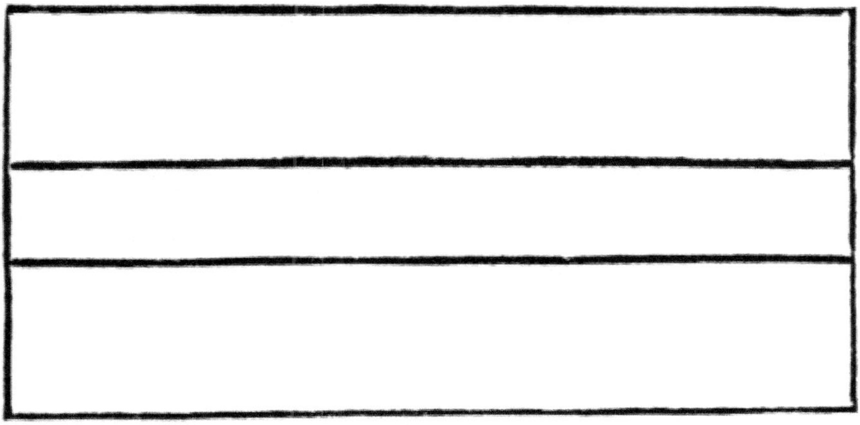

Fig. 1.

Lorgnettes are very easy indeed, and are a neat design. Fold the serviette in half lengthways. Fold back an inch, or an inch and a half, at the double end, and bring it to the centre, in the same way observable in fig. 1. Turn it over on the other side and roll both ends, one at a time, to the centre; taking care to press in with the fingers, as it is rolled, the tendency is to bag up; so as to keep it smooth outside, and the centre band tight. Stand it upright. The Lorgnettes do not inclose the bread.

Fig. 2.

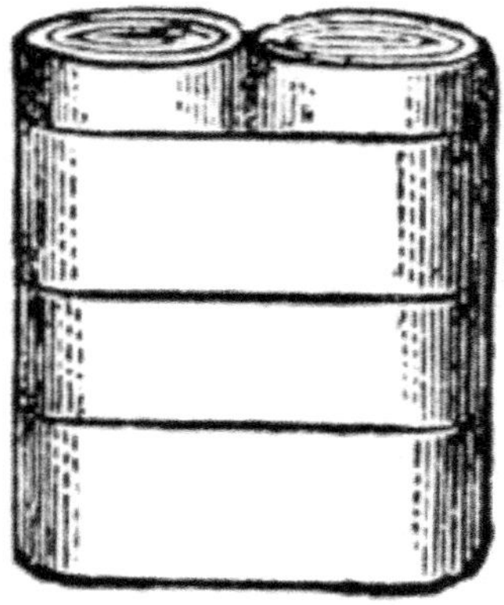

Fig. 3.

THE PYRAMID.

The Pyramid, provided the napkin is very stiff and fine, is easily made. Double it in half one side within an inch of the other, so that it may be more slender towards the point. Fold it in seven the narrow way, like fig. 3, in the shell. Press these folds down with an iron; then crimp them across with a paper knife, folding it in and out the width of the knife. Lastly, join it round like a pyramid, and stand it upright over the bread. For a bride, or a distinguished guest, slender wreaths of flowers may be placed all round in every crimping.

THE FLEUR-DE-LYS.

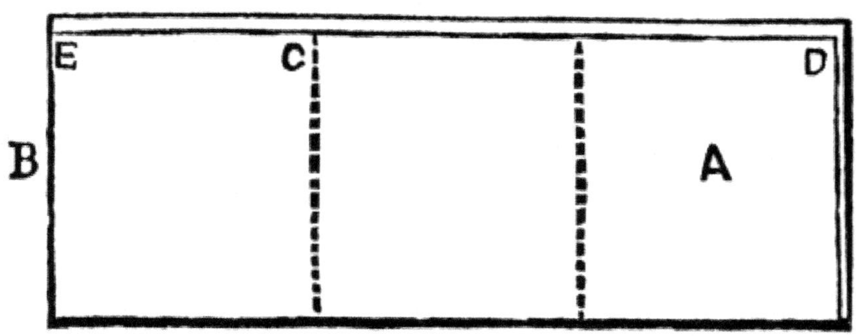

Fig. 1.

The Fleur-de-Lys should be folded with very stiff damask, a little damp, and fresh ironed; but may be made with a small light damask, without starch, by using a little pin at the back of the waist, marked C to

D in diagram (fig. 5). Rich heavy damask of a large size is always tiresome to fold without starch, although looking whiter, brighter, and handsomer on table. Lay the serviette flat on the table: fold it in half; and in half again, lengthwise; keeping the selvages all to the top. Halve it the narrow way, A to B (fig. 1). Merely make the crease, and open this last fold again: thus you have the centre marked. Take the ends E and D, and fold them to the centre: you thus have an oblong, equal to two squares. Turn down the corner E, and you have a resemblance to fig. 2. Take the point D in that diagram, and bring it to C. Take the point E and turn it under to C, in the way shown in fig. 3. Treat the point F in the same manner. Thus fig. 4 is made. Double fig. 4 in half, flat from A to B. Hold it tight between the thumb and finger at C and D. Take hold of the points at A and pull them out to resemble the petals of a Fleur-de-Lys, like fig. 5. Turn up the corners, E and F, at right angles to stand it upon, pinching the waist well in. If not quite stiff enough to stand alone, after being pinched a moment, place a pin at the back of the waist; but pins are always better avoided.

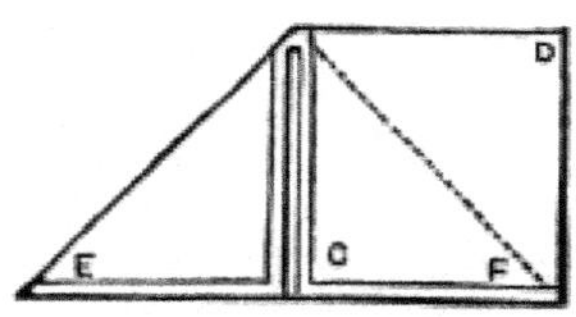

Fig. 2.

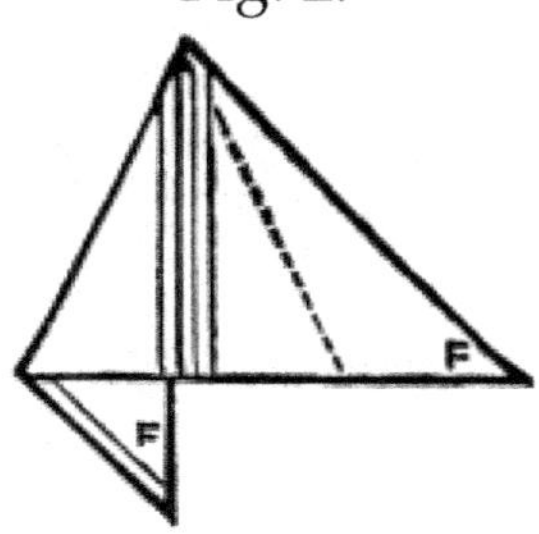

Fig. 3.

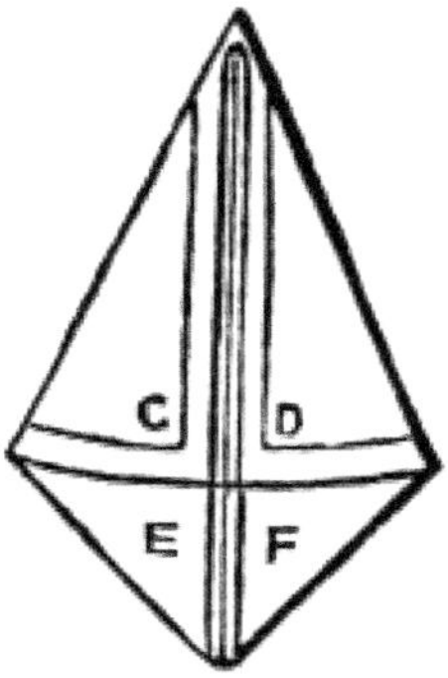

Fig. 4.

Fig. 5.

THE ARCHBISHOP'S, OR DOUBLE MITRE.

The Archbishop's, or Double Mitre, is exceedingly pretty, and may be folded from any serviette. First fold the linen in half, and lay it flat on the table. Turn down six inches from the top. Fold down an inch and a half of this at the edge, and fold that over again; the folds forming an outside band like that shown in fig. 1, from A to B. Raise the ends A and B in the hand, and form the point C, in fig. 2, allowing the folds of the linen to overlap a little. Smooth it down flat, without raising or moving it from the table; fold the lower end the same, and bring it up to D E, in fig. 3. Turn the fold D E, down on the right side, and make another point with it like that at C, in fig. 2, but a little lower, so as to show the top point above it. Lastly, fold up the lower edge F G, about an inch and a half, to form the band of the Mitre. Bring the two ends F and G, round to the back, to make the shape of a cap, and insert one in the other. If large enough, fit it over the dinner roll. If not, set it on the table, and place the roll upright in the hollow. The front should face the guest.

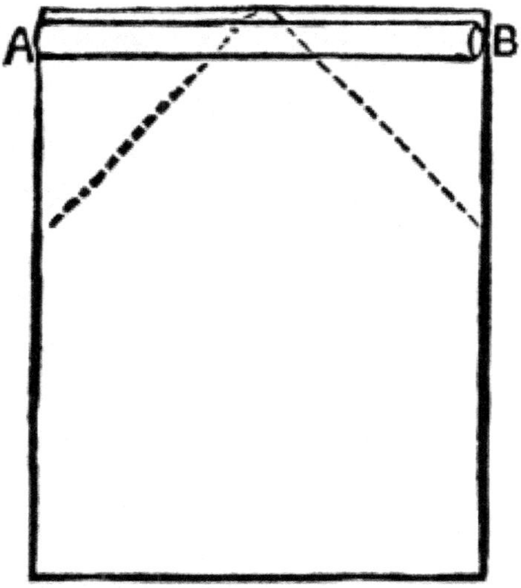

Fig. 1.

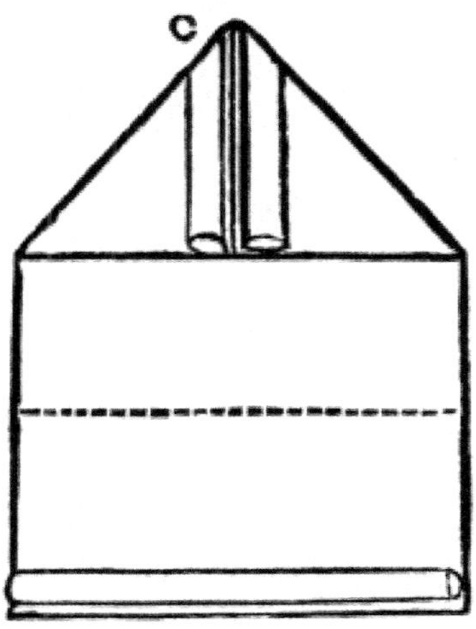

Fig. 2.

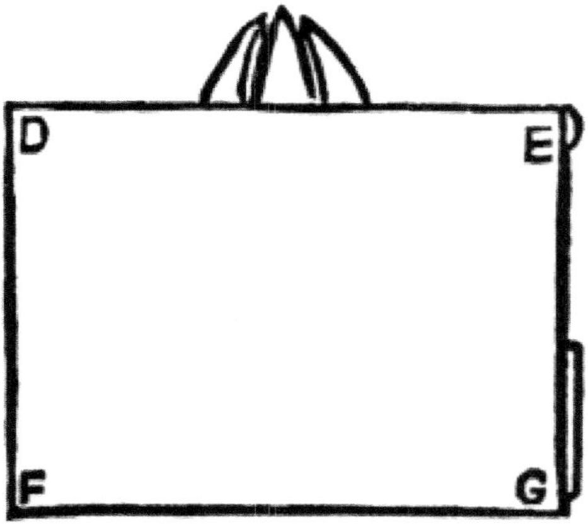

Fig. 3.

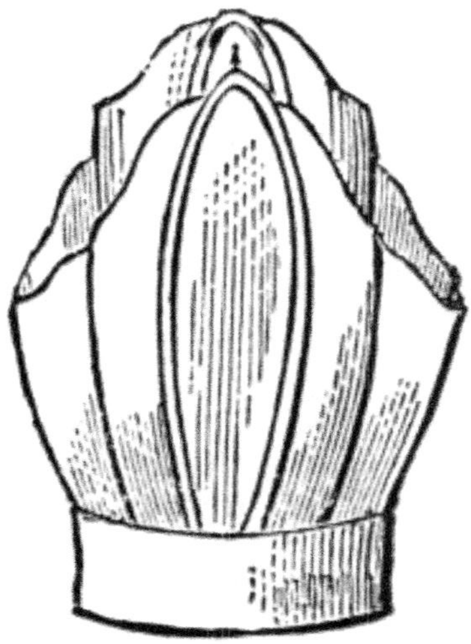

THE BREAD BASKET.

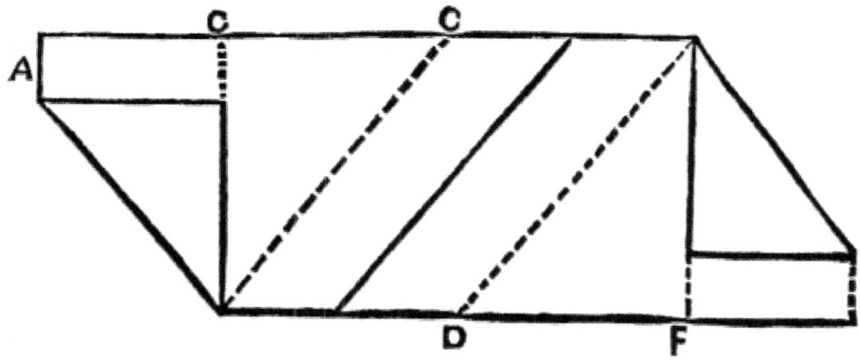

Fig. 1.

Fold the serviette four times lengthways. Turn down the corners in the way observed in fig. 1. Make the three standing folds across the centre, the middle one to project, C and D to bend inwards. This makes a hill or ridge in the centre. Fold back each corner at the dotted lines F and C. Now hold it erect like fig. 2. Pinch it up together in a flat line. Make a circle of it by bringing the ends together and inserting B in A. Place it round the bread.

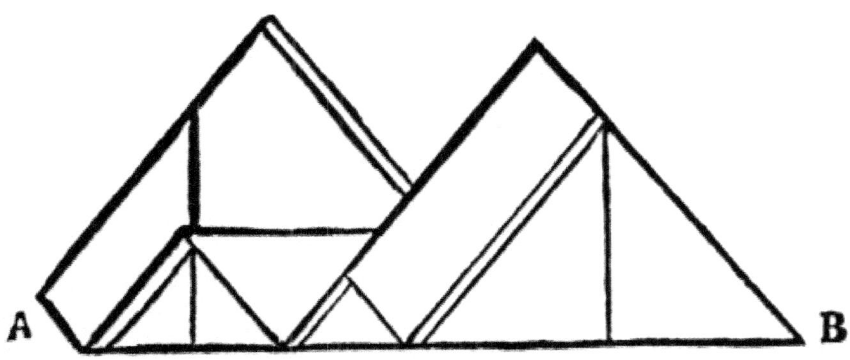

Fig. 2.

THE FLOWER BASKET.

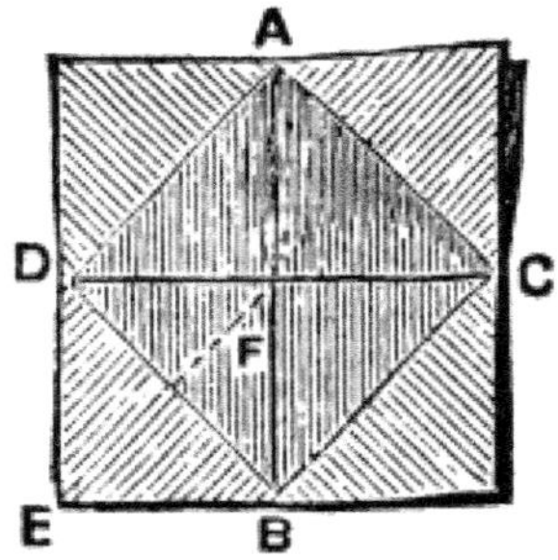

Fig. 1.

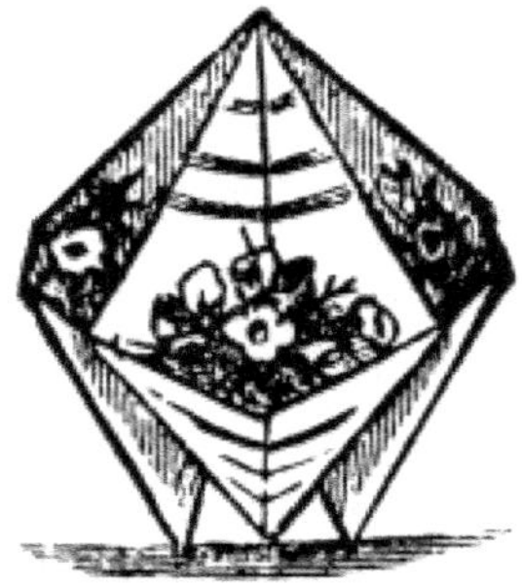

Fig. 2.

Fig. 3.

Take a very stiff square of damask, and fold it exactly in half. Open and fold in half the reverse way. The centre is now ascertained. Fold all the corners very exactly to the centre. Iron them down; turn over, and again turn the corners to the centre. Turn the serviette over again and take each corner from the centre, and fold it back at the half. Then crease it from A to B (fig. 1), open the crease, and fold it again from C to D. Take it in the hand and bring the crease A to C, and C to B, and so all round. This will enable you to make it stand. Hold the apex between the fingers of one hand and square out the four sides. This makes it resemble fig. 2, and completes it. A few flowers should be arranged in the compartments. For variety the corners may be left upright, like fig. 3. By reversing it, as shown in fig. 4, a different design is obtained.

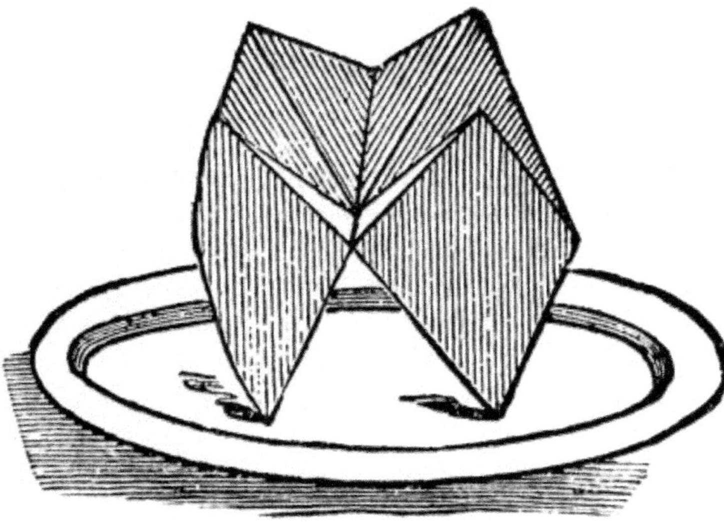

Fig. 4.

THE IMPERIAL CROWN.

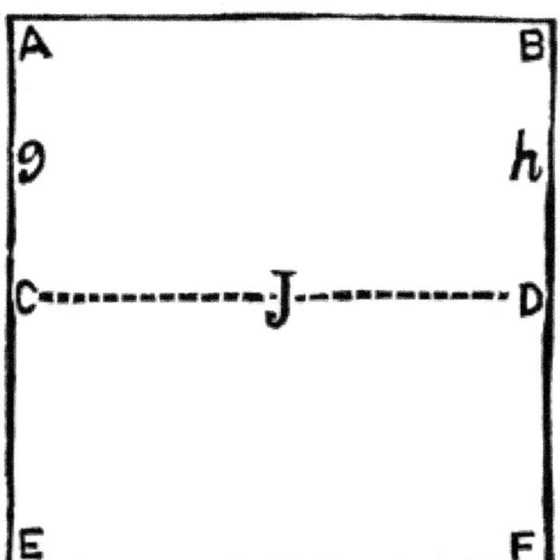

Fig. 1.

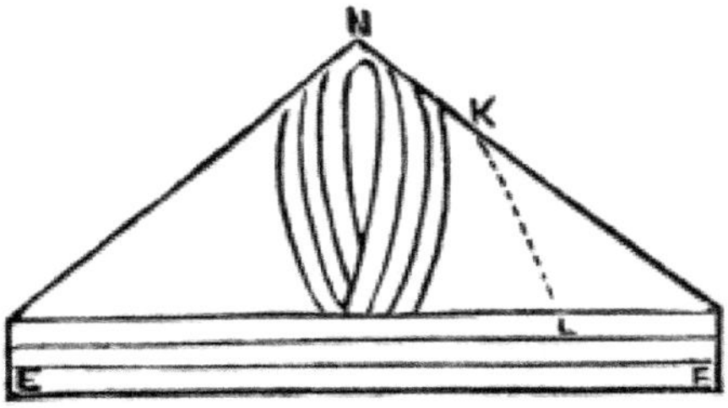

Fig. 2.

The Imperial Crown requires very stiff damask--an exact square is best,--and either a very small serviette, or a very large one folded in four, to reduce it to a quarter its size. Lay it flat on the table: fold the end, A, B, over to the dotted line in the centre, C D. Do the same the other side, bringing E F to C D. Then place the end, A B, in three folds, as for a fan, the whole length of the damask, and crease them down, making the folds exactly use the piece between A B, and the fold at *g*, *h*. Then fold the end, E F, to match. Then bring the folded ends, A B, to the centre, *j*, crossing the folded part of one over the other where they meet. The serviette will now look like fig. 2. Turn the fold, E F, to the back and fold down. Next bring the corner E, by the dotted line K J, completely across, like fig. 3; the end N is to be level with the end E. The end N is then to be crossed over to match, and the end of the band inserted in the folds of the other, so as to hold firmly together. Put the hand inside and shape it. When set over the dinner roll it will stand firm. It should be a full-sized roll. The front of the hat should face the guest. If the *carte de menu* is not too large, it may be placed in the plaited fold at N, before crossing the ends over.

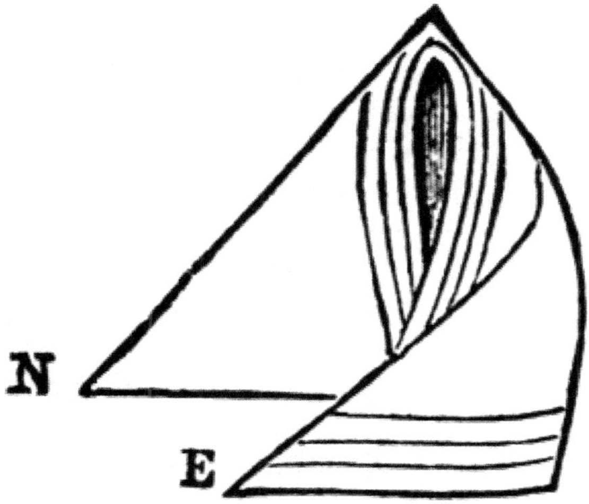

Fig. 3.

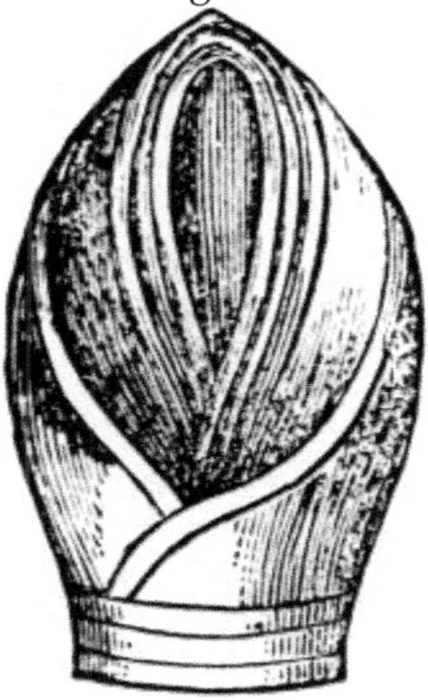

Fig. 4.

THE DOUBLE HORN OF PLENTY.

This requires a stiff serviette, damp and fresh ironed. It may, however, be made from a limp one, if a small pin is inserted at each side, after the last fold. Lay the serviette flat on the table; fold in four lengthwise, keeping all the selvages one way. Turn the two ends to meet in the centre. Turn that over, and turn down two corners not at the selvage edge, at the lines A to B, and C to D. Turn it over and it will resemble fig.

1. Take the end C, and roll it over to D (see fig. 2). Bring A to B in the same manner, and complete the design. It is most suitable for a Christmas dinner party, when it may be filled with holly or any bright flowers; or one space may be filled with holly and the other with grapes, almonds, raisins, &c., to represent plenty (see fig. 3). Pinch the horns down and hold them a minute, to make them preserve their shape.

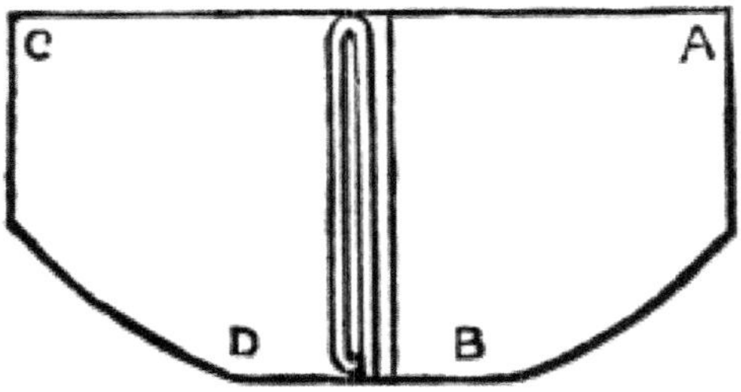

Fig. 1.

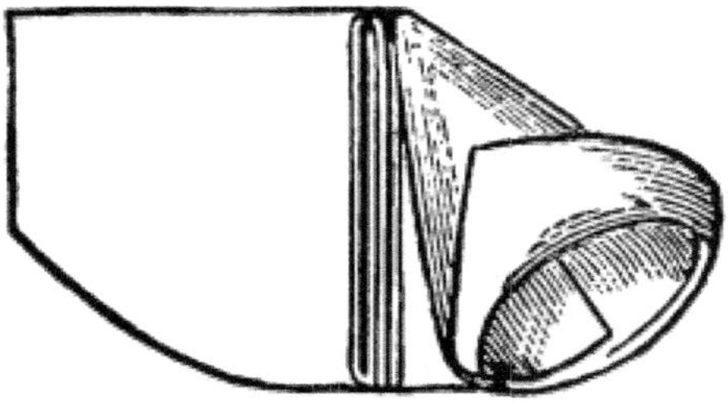

Fig. 2.

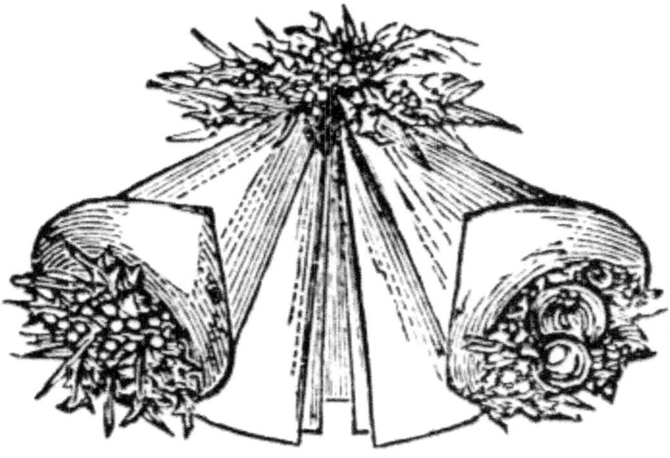

Fig. 3.

THE COLONNE DE TRIOMPHE.

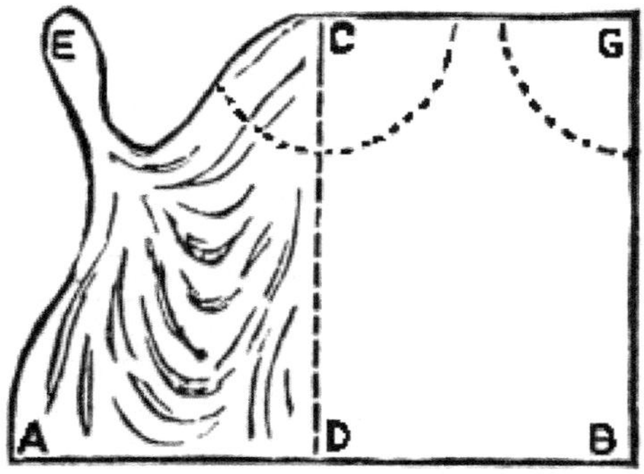

Fig. 1.

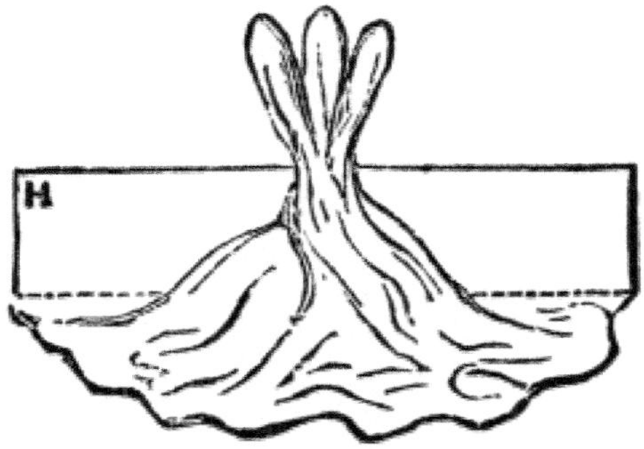

Fig. 2.

Fig. 3.

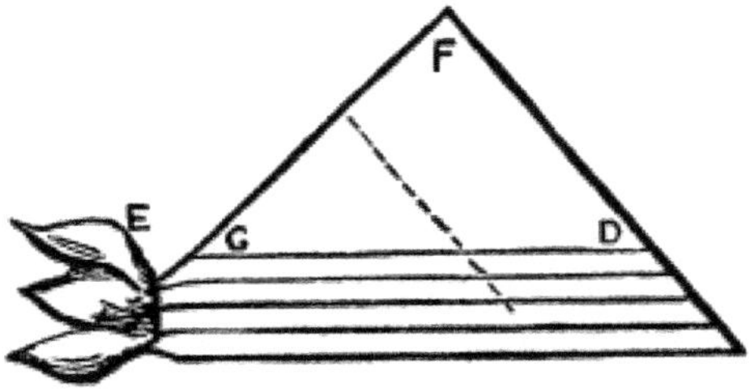

Fig. 4.

Fig. 5.

This is difficult to fold, although it may be done with a soft damask. Starch is, however, an improvement. The secret of success depends entirely on rolling it *very* lightly. Lay the serviette flat on the table. From A to B (fig. 1), fold down about six inches, if it is a large serviette. After trying the fold once, by reference the illustration, it will be seen if the proportion is properly kept. The one which we have just folded ourselves, as a model, stands fifteen inches high, eleven for the shaft of the column, and it is very erect and firm, although made of limp damask. Fold the damask in half from C to D (fig. 1), to ascertain the half. In the left hand nip up the corner E, as shown in the illustration; the centre C and the corner G in the same way, like fig. 2, shaping them into laurel leaves. Then pleat down the serviette, holding the top still in the hand, in the way described in fig. 3. Next take the end H (fig. 2), that is, the left hand lower corner, and pass it completely round the serviette to the right, bringing the selvage tight around A to B in fig. 3. Lay it on the table, holding the neck at E grasped in the hand, at first; and tucking down and keeping tight the folds from C to D (fig. 4), whilst rolling over the end E to F, as tightly as possible, umbrella wise; pressing it on the table as you roll it up, to keep it firm. Fasten the end with a little pin. Then firmly tuck in the odd corners at the base, in the way half a pound of sugar or an ounce of almonds are turned in. Twine a wreath of flowers around it. The artificial wreaths of small roses or holly, sold at the grocers', are pretty for the purpose. Set it upright, and with a little manipulation it will sit firm in the plate.

THE TULIP.

The Tulip requires a very stiff material. The folds are very simple, but requires nicety of fingering and pressure with a hot iron. Bring all the corners to the centre, as for the Crown. Bring the corners down to the centre again and again; in all five times. Press it well. Finish all the serviettes to be folded so far, and then recommence with the first by turning down all the corners one by one, to form the Tulip petals, which should hang down in long points, like a dog's ears. Place the Tulip on a glass.

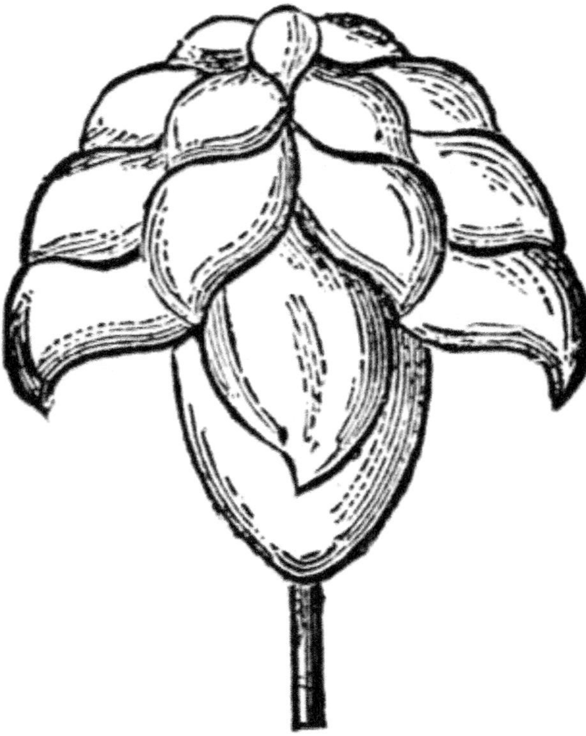

THE BRIDAL SERVIETTE.

Fig. 1.

Fig. 2.

The Bridal Serviette is almost identical with the Pyramid, and is so called because it is a favorite for wedding breakfasts. At the top it is to be decorated with a few flowers. For the bride, stephanotis, white roses, or any white flowers available, mixed with a little orange blossom. For the other guests a scarlet flower. The serviette must be very stiff and damp from fresh ironing. Lay it on the table flat. Fold it not in half, but within an inch and a half of the top (see fig. 1). Take the corners A and B, and fold them to C and D again, within an inch and a half of the last fold, and like the last fold flat and straight across. This produces fig. 2. Again take the ends E and F and fold over to G and H, within an inch and a half of the last fold. This will probably about halve the remaining piece; but that will depend on the size of the serviette. Then fold it the narrow way, backwards and forwards, as for a fan, nine times, creasing it firmly down. Opening it as little as possible, turn down all the tops of the folds in the way noticed in fig. 3, beginning at the top of the three tiers. Then join it round, fixing the first fold over the last, and pinch it together at the top.

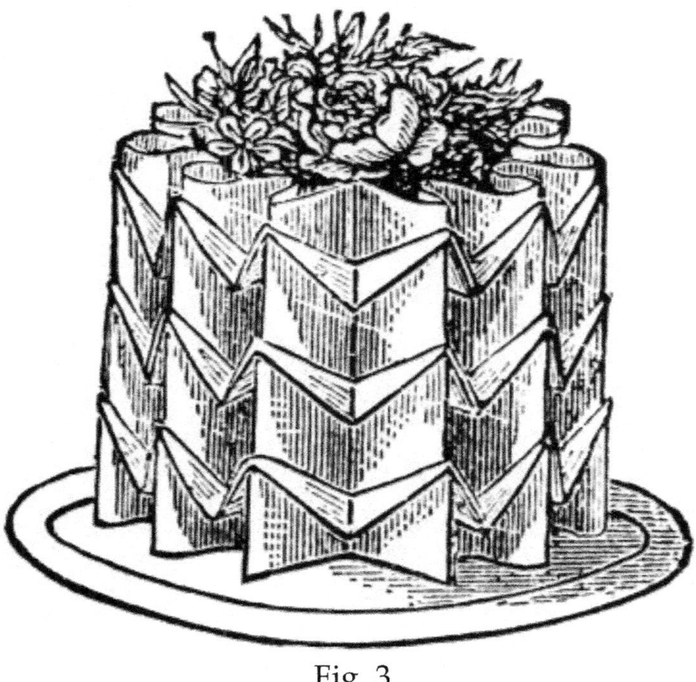

Fig. 3.

THE PRINCE OF WALES'S FEATHER.

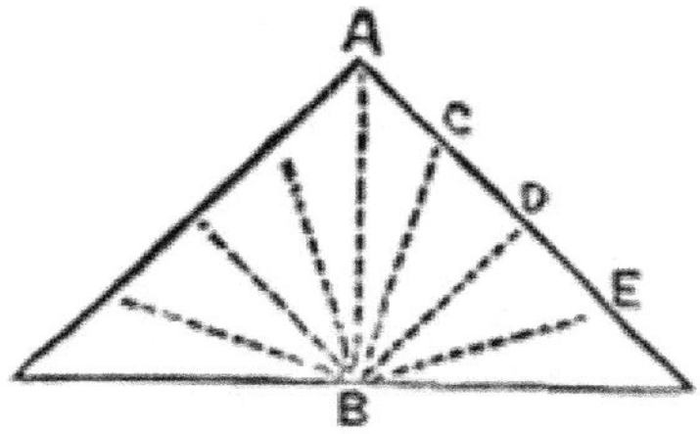

Fig. 1.

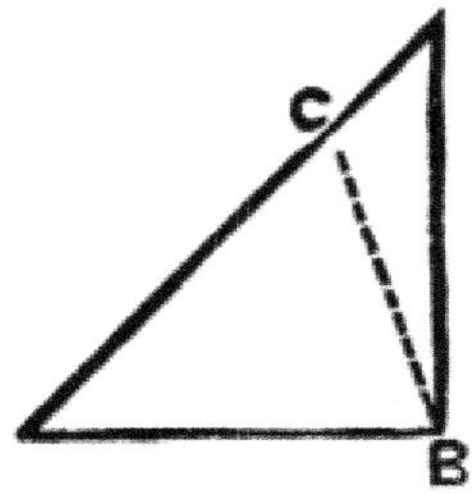

Fig. 2.

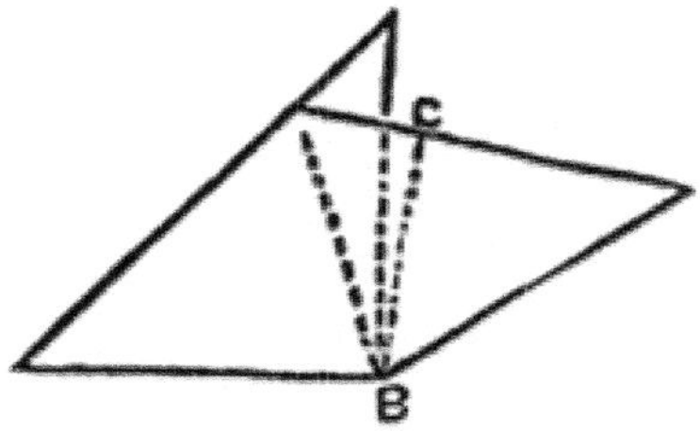

Fig. 3.

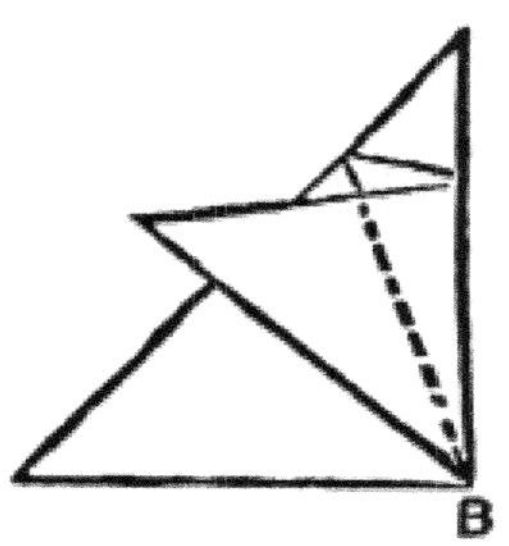

Fig. 4.

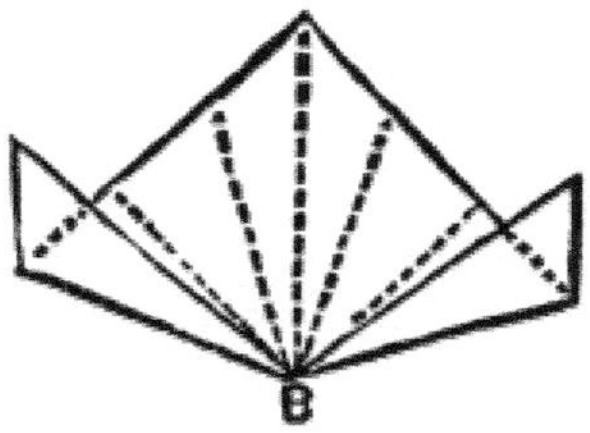

Fig. 5.

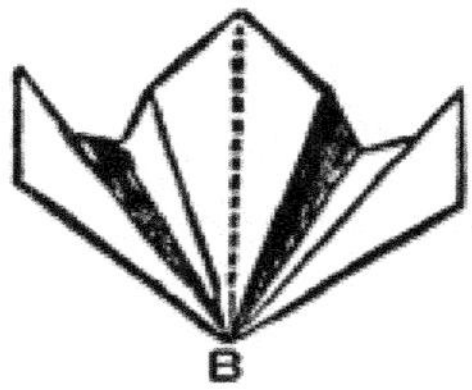

Fig. 6.

The Prince of Wales's Feather is a perfectly new design, invented especially for the present work. It is simple in effect and very handsome in appearance. It requires a very stiff crisp serviette. Lay the damask on the table, ironing it damp. Fold it from fig. 2 in the Crown, from A to B, using the hot iron to crease it. Without disturbing this fold, crease in half again the reverse way, from C to D, thus reducing the size to a quarter. Smooth it with the iron. Next fold this in half diagonally, like fig. 4 in the Crown. Observe fig. 4, in the illustrations on the present page, carefully. Fold it in half from A to B, using the iron; this will produce fig. 2. Make the fold C to B, on one side only, in the manner shown in fig. 3. Then fold it back again at the dotted line D, and it will resemble fig. 4. Fold the other side to match, always using the iron to press every fold. Open it and it will resemble fig. 5, with the folds A, C, D. Make the folds, E, as shown in fig. 5, taking care not to flatten the other folds, leaving the serviette only just open enough to make the folds, E, each side. It now resembles fig. 6. Bring the last two folds quite flat and inside C and D, and it will resemble fig. 7. Treat the other side the same, and then fold it in half in the middle, A, and it will resemble fig. 8. Now allow it to open a little and hold it by the apex, B, fig. 9. Keep it very much indented in the centre (A to B); bring the wings or side feathers forward, and curl over the three lips of the feather by bending them with the fingers. Place it upright in a wine glass or a slender single flower glass in the same manner as the Fan is placed. Fig. 10 shows the Prince of Wales's Feather complete.

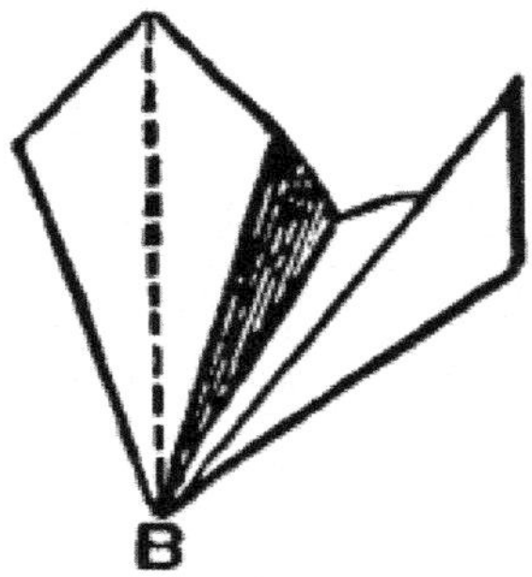

Fig. 7.

Fig. 8.

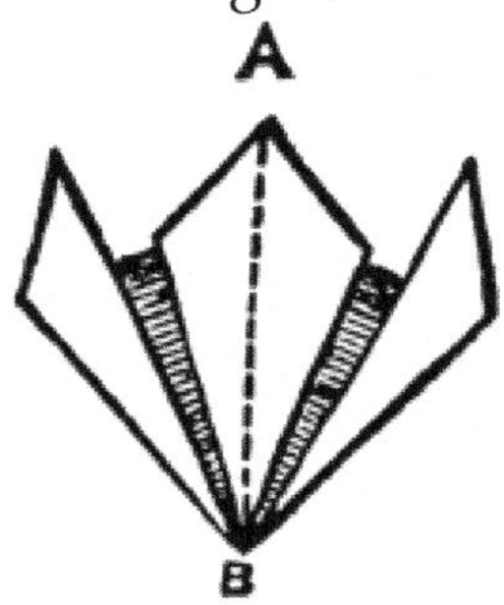

Fig. 9.

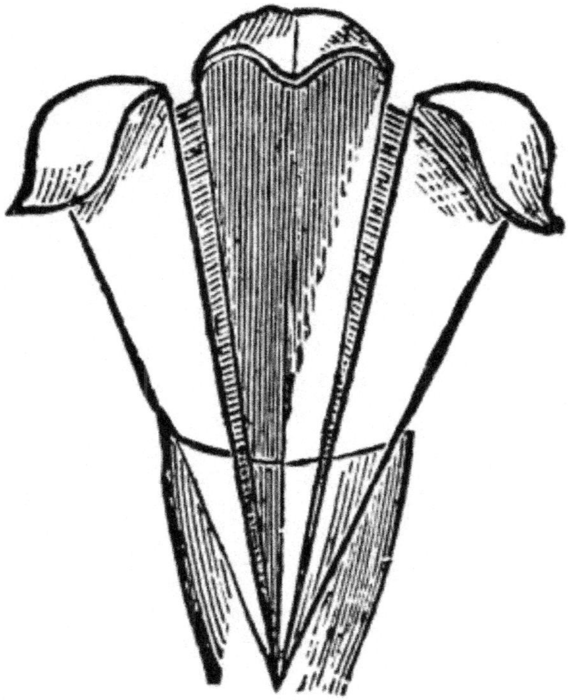

Fig. 10.

THE END

Printed in Dunstable, United Kingdom

77168342R00037